Winter Camping

Winter Camping

Bob Cary

WITH
ILLUSTRATIONS BY THE AUTHOR

The Stephen Greene Press

BRATTLEBORO, VERMONT

This book has been produced in the United States of America.
It is designed by R. L. Dothard Associates and published by The Stephen Greene Press, Brattleboro, Vermont 05301.

LIBRARY OF CONGRESS CATALOGING IN PUBLICATION DATA:

Cary, Bob.
    Winter camping.

    Includes index.
    1. Snow camping.   2. Camping.   I. Title
GV198.9.C37   796.5′4   78-58680
ISBN 0-8289-0339-5
ISBN 0-8289-0340-9 pbk.

Contents

Preface

There is, in the general public's mind, something which associates winter camping with winter survival. That is not what this book is about. Survival implies existing through a harrowing ordeal that resulted from an accident or a mistake. This book is not written for people hunting that kind of trouble. It is a compilation of tested cold weather camping procedures for the growing number of skiers, snowshoers and campers who seek to add another dimension to their sheer enjoyment of the outdoors.

Much of the information involving equipment and methods contained in this book, comes from the extensive winter program conducted at the Charles Sommers Wilderness Canoe Base, located twenty-two miles east of Ely, Minnesota, on the edge of the Boundary Waters Canoe Area. This winter adventure, named "Okpik," the Inuit name for the snowy owl, currently provides snow camping experience for 700 to 800 young men and women each year through the High Adventure Program of the Boy Scouts of America. The base staff, including a dozen winter guides, also functions as a radio-directed search-and-rescue team for the entire midsection of the 2,000 square-mile Boundary Waters area. Over the years during which this program has been developing, Resident Director Sandy Bridges has used the base as a center for coordinating cold weather operational information. He has gathered material from the Canadian Armed Forces and the U.S. Army, Navy and Air Force, and has tapped the vast fund of experience of north-country guides, trappers, ice fishermen, hunters, recreational skiers, sled-dog mushers and U.S. Forest Service personnel. The Sommers base has served as an extensive testing site for hundreds of items of zero weather military and recreational equipment and as an experimental laboratory in which winter equipment is designed, made and tested.

Key to the winter program has been the development of the unique "cross-country sled," a very light, boat-type equipment carrier with a slick outer shell which glides through the snow with a minimum of resistance. The sled was designed and built by Erling Hegg of Togo, Minnesota. Several models are now in production and are becoming widely used for recreational winter camping as well as expedition work. The sled allows the load to be pulled, rather than carried on the shoulders, an arrangement which makes it possible for even youngsters to participate in winter trips without the strain and fatigue caused by carrying heavy backpacks.

It has been this writer's good fortune to live just up the shore from the Sommers Base and to be associated with the Okpik operation both as an advisor and a learner and as part of the search-and-rescue program. For several years, Sandy Bridges and I were co-teachers in the Winter Guide Training Program authorized by the Minnesota Department of Education at Duluth, Eveleth and Ely. We have also had the opportunity to meet with many cold weather authorities, both military and civilian, and with equipment designers. In addition, we have researched extensively the journals of North American explorers, gleaning information from their experiences in snow travel. This book is based on ideas and methods gathered from this multiplicity of sources and tested extensively in sub-zero weather.

Bob Cary

Ely, Minnesota
September, 1978

1: The Fun of Winter Camping

We are born furless and fragile, a species basically equipped for living in a moderately warm climate. The fact that humans have not only penetrated the most hostile arctic regions, but have lived there comfortably for centuries, is a tribute to the insatiable curiosity, the adaptability and the ingenuity of the species. Man is the only creature who can create his own environment and haul it with him.

The hunters came first. The prototypes of our present skis, snowshoes, sleds, shelters, bedding and insulated clothing were developed centuries ago by hunters who pursued game over snow and ice, ranging further and further north as they observed, learned and adapted. It was not out of necessity that they established residence in the north, but out of choice. They enjoyed it. Certainly the Inuit, the people we know as Eskimos, are among

the most happy, fun-loving people on earth and they consider their lives anything but precarious. While few of us will probably sample winter camping in the arctic, the Inuit formula for cold weather living is basic: Don't fight winter; learn to live with it.

WHAT DOES IT TAKE?

Winter camping is not summer camping in long underwear. The equipment is different, the methods are different, the medium is different. Those of us who guide and/or teach in cold weather programs in the North have been long concerned over the lack of good information on snow camping. Some of us who serve on search-and-rescue teams have seen the results of challenging winter with the wrong equipment and methods. The summer backpacker or canoeist who goes out with a poor outfit, or who loses some of his gear or even himself, may get rain-soaked and bug-bitten while he is getting out of his predicament. But in the winter, with temperatures ranging from zero to 45 below, mistakes are an unaffordable luxury. A performance grade of C or D is not passing in the winter. There are only straight A's.

Equipment

Specialists in quality backpacking gear are designing and building tents for cold weather use which can be readily adapted for summer camping. The same is true of some items of bedding, cooking and clothing. However, not much typical summer camping equipment can be adapted to winter use. This fact is something to bear in mind when considering a purchase.

Skills

Most winter camping is done by skiers or snowshoers who wish to make more extended trips or by backpackers who simply hate to give up their sport because the seasons change. These trail pushers generally stay physically fit and have considerable stamina along with the ability to adapt and learn quickly. The county campground visitor with his tent trailer and propane ice box is not under discussion here. There is nothing wrong with that type of camping, but the self-propelled snow camper is a different breed of cat.

The camper who operates out of the tailgate of his station wagon can haul along an almost unlimited supply of equipment aimed at transporting as much of his home environment as possible into the outdoors. The winter camper, on the other hand, moving his outfit through the snow with his legs and back, is extremely weight conscious. Any item which is not essential is not packed. Generations of snow travellers have developed the slogan: "Keep it simple." Nobody has improved on that concept.

It should not be necessary to point out that a working acquaintance with skis or snowshoes is essential to winter camping. Nevertheless, every year we see a good number of backpackers in the North who have somehow gotten the idea that they can slog through three feet of powder on nothing but Vibram soles. We also see some groups come apart at the seams because a member has decided he will learn how to ski or snowshoe "on the trip."

We have no exact data, but we feel that it takes three times more effort to negotiate slopes and twisting forest trails with a pack and sled than it does on skis or snowshoes alone. This is an unrealistic and unsafe burden to place on a beginner. The trip should be tailored to fit the ability of the campers, or the campers should be carefully selected by skill and experience to match the length and difficulty of the trip.

Attitude

Many campers we meet on the north-country trails in the summer admit that they have thought about winter camping but are "afraid" of what it entails. Such fear can be based only on a lack of information or an oversupply of misinformation. The winter camper does not "fear" the cold any more than the skier "fears" a steep downhill run or the backpacker "fears" the mountain. Cold is simply an ingredient necessary for snow. Certainly the snow traveller respects his environment. He does not look on the trip as an ordeal or a test, however, but as a learning experience. For the experienced snow camper, the only danger in snow camping is getting addicted to it. If you are on a summer trip, slogging up a rain-soaked, mosquito-inhabited trail and your imagination spawns an expanse of sparkling snow, laced with long dark shadows from towering spruce that jam white-capped fingers into a limitless blue sky . . . my friend, you are hooked.

Ethics

There are far fewer real effects from camping on forest trails and campsites in the winter than in the summer. It is next to impossible in the winter to start a forest fire, and it is relatively difficult to hack down live trees, peel birch, cause trail erosion or destroy campsites. On the other hand, while it is easy to bury trash and waste under the snow, it is reborn the moment spring arrives. Anything that is not burned should be packed out. It is essential that the snow camper carefully observe the camping ethic of the summer backpacker and canoeist, that he camp and leave no sign of occupancy. The only indication of his passing should be prints in the snow that vanish with the spring thaw.

A big difference between summer and winter camping is in respect to open fires. In warm weather camping, when cooking is done over a wood fire, emphasis is placed on keeping the fire small and using a minimum of fuel. In the winter, it is often desirable to get a fire going to dry out gear and warm up people, something a tiny cook fire will not accomplish. In winter camping, nearly all cooking is done on a small stove, but a heat-producing wood fire nearby is a welcome addition. Many trips are made without using open fires because of preference, lack of available wood or government regulations on fire building. But where wood is available, a good fire is a plus. Like the summer camper, the winter traveller scatters his charcoal and smooths out the site so that little indication of a fire is left.

Briefly, in this chapter, we have covered some of the ingredients which go into the sport of winter camping. We have attempted to lead the reader from venturing out of a permanent, centrally heated home for a few hours of fun in the snow to a world in which he will haul his shelter with him and become a part of the winter environment for days or even weeks. In the following chapters we will spell out the details which make this challenging transition not only possible, but enjoyable.

1: The Fun of Winter Camping

2: Packing in the Outfit

Occasionally one encounters a winter camping article in a magazine which leads off with a color photo showing some bearded adventurer poised on the brink of a snow-capped precipice, skis aimed downward, bulging scarlet expedition frame pack towering high above his shoulders. It is an impressive picture. More impressive if one has not tried it.

Even on hard pack, the weight of a high backpack creates a very difficult balancing act, so difficult that the skier or snowshoer spends a good deal of his time digging himself out of drifts. In typical deep forest snow, the would-be camper discovers that there is no fun in trying to break trail with that additional weight on his back pushing him into the powder up to his crotch. He starts to look for a better way. And he doesn't have to look far.

Native dwellers of the north discovered centuries ago that it is far easier and quicker to pull a load over the snow in a sled or toboggan than it is to backpack it. Either those of us of European descent are slow learners or we are less than observant, because it has only been in recent years that the recreational winter camper has been getting the load off his back. Perhaps we just didn't have the right sled available . . . but we do now.

CROSS–COUNTRY SLED

Veteran skier and winter camper Erling Hegg of Togo, Minnesota, began building one-man, lightweight fiberglass sleds more than a decade ago. The originals were narrow, flatbottom models pulled with a rope. The newer models built by his Nord Hus firm are highly functional pieces of art. They are in use from Minnesota to Alaska and Baffinland.

The sleds are 48 inches long with a 19½ inch beam and 5 inch depth. They taper from 10 inches in front to 18 inches at the rear and have a built-in deck projecting 10 inches back from the bow. Total weight is 10 pounds.

Hegg makes some special expedition sleds which are 8 feet long

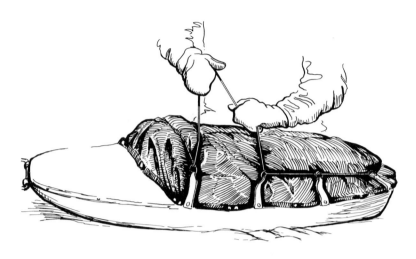

The one-man fiberglass cross-country sled: key to winter camping.

and can haul nearly 250 pounds. These sleds were used on the 52-day Ellesmere Island trip by Neal Gillette, Doug Wiens, Allan Bard and Chuck Schultz. The trip originated on April 15, 1977, and covered 450 miles via cross-country skis with no air drops or preplanned caches, and without the aid of either machines or dogs. This carefully planned and beautifully executed arctic adventure was accomplished by each man pulling a Hegg sled loaded with 240 pounds of duffle and food. That is, the load weighed that much at the start. Food declined at a rate of three pounds per day per sled, which meant that the skiers literally ate their way to lightness. It should be noted that these men were no novices. Gillette and Wiens are veteran skiers from the Trapp Family Lodge in Vermont. Bard instructs at the Yosemite Mountaineering School, Yosemite, California, and Chuck Schultz is with the Robbins Mountain Shop, Modesto, California. Furthermore, for ordinary winter camping, the big sleds and heavy loads are not necessary.

Earlier Hegg sleds were designed so that goods and equipment could be wrapped inside a tarp and lashed in. The new models come with an integral nylon cover riveted to the sides. The cover folds over the outfit and is secured with elastic cord laced through four snaps and four grommets. The snaps are all on one side, allow-

2: *Packing in the Outfit*

The cross-country sled allows beginners, children and others for whom winter camping has been impracticable to pack in the needed gear and supplies.

ing instant release of the lashing in order to reach any item of equipment inside. This hookup is designed so that the lashing can be tied down or released easily by the camper without taking off his mittens.

The Gelcoat cover on the Hegg sled's hull is so slick and hard that it requires no waxing or other preparation. The sled's strength in proportion to its weight is remarkable. And not only do sleds provide a fast vehicle for moving equipment, but they make excellent tables when turned upside down at the campsite.

Cross-country sleds are available from Nord Hus, P.O. Box 4, Togo, Minn., 55788. Prices are: $130 for the four-footer, $165 for the six-footer and $250 for the eight-foot expedition model. These prices include a complete set of shafts and shoulder harness.

The only other type of winter cargo carrier available is the toboggan, used for centuries by northern Indians and still used by tough woodsmen to move supplies. Compared to the cross-country sled, the toboggan is slow, easily broken, difficult to steer, hard to pull in deep snow and not much fun, particularly for youngsters or novices. Quality toboggans such as Snowcraft run $54 for a six-footer, $67 for an eight-footer.

Harness

Some cross-country sled models used for two-man snowshoe travel are still rigged with bow and stern ropes for uphill–downhill mobility. But the standard harness for the cross-country sled, one which works equally well with skis or snowshoes, is built on two fiberglass poles inserted into aluminum "U" frames. This straps to the sled, creating a flexible tow rig seventy-eight inches long. The pole harness prevents the sled from overrunning the skier or snow-shoer going downhill and also provides maximum lateral control. The harness buckles at the hip with a wide nylon band. Springs on each side act as shock absorbers against the pull of the load. Some campers have added a chest strap to relieve some of the pull at the hips. While the harness is serviceable, it is still undergoing

Belt hitch of cross-country sled harness showing spring-loaded shock absorber for smoothing the pull of the loaded sled.

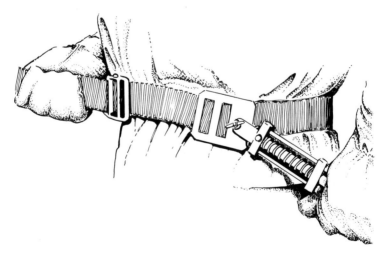

The cross-country sled in use.

modification. Some models are now being built with quick-release buckles, which are an advantage in getting in and out of the harness.

Only on steep grades or when breaking trail in heavy snow is one conscious of having the cross-country sled in tow. On hard pack or good trail there is scarcely any sensation of pulling.

Packing the Sled

Attention to balancing the load adds to the cross-country sled's performance. We pack the sled with the weight centered slightly toward the rear to provide bow "lift" in addition to the upward pull of the harness. Because weight and bulk are not nearly as critical in a sled as in a backpack, a few luxuries can be included with the necessities. Here is a breakdown of our sled list:

Tent, poles and anchors
Kitchen fly, extra tarps

Insulated boots and extra clothing

Loading the sled: heavy items on bottom.

Extra rope	First aid kit
Stove	Ice fishing gear
Shovel	Toilet kit
Snow knife	Candles
Lantern	Reading material
Mantles	Repair kit
Fuel	Paper towelling
Funnel	Matches
Food	Flashlight, extra batteries
Cook kit pots and utensils	Extra ski tips, ski wax, snow-
Folding saw	shoes
Ice chisel	Foam sleeping pads

We start loading the cross-country sled by laying out all of the gear alongside the sled, making sure there is no snow inside and taking care to brush off the items as they are loaded. Food is usually packed in one or two sturdy cardboard boxes narrow enough to fit easily inside the sled. We pack the lantern in a cardboard carton, padded to protect the glass chimney. Heavy, bulky items such as the food, tent, lantern and fuel are laid inside first. The fuel can is checked for tightness. Long items such as the ice chisel, tent

2: *Packing in the Outfit*

poles and ice fishing rods are laid alongside the boxes. The ice chisel is sheathed and so is an axe if one is taken. The rest of the gear is packed to round off the top of the load so that there are no edges to catch brush or branches, no parts of the nylon cover projecting where wear can occur, and no sharp items pushing against the cover to cause a puncture or rip. The last item put in is the shovel, so that it will be the first item available at camp.

With all items in place, the nylon cover is folded over and secured with the elastic cord. On top of the load we lash an extra pair of snowshoes, useful for trail packing in deep snow if you are travelling on skis or in case of emergency breakage if you are on snowshoes. Admittedly, there are a lot of cross-country skiers who would rather be caught dead than seen on snowshoes, but carrying snowshoes is good insurance in forested, soft-snow territory. In camp they are handy for hustling firewood and for stamping out a tent platform if it is not possible to dig down to solid earth. A spare ski pole is also carried, since poles are used in both ski and snowshoe travelling.

BACKPACKS

The only items that go on our backs are sleeping gear and, when we are on skis, the wax bag and an extra ski tip. Synthetic fiber or

Backpack on pack frame. Foam sleeping mat strapped on top of load.

down winter bags are light but bulky and take up room on the sled that is needed for heavier items. We prefer small frame mountaineering packs which can be snugged down, keep the weight low, and will not swing from side to side. The total weight of the pack and sleeping outfit will run somewhere around ten pounds, depending on the make and material. This is a balanceable load which will not interfere with normal skiing or snowshoeing. Any time the pack gets to twenty pounds or over it presents a balance problem.

THE CROSS–COUNTRY SLED WITH SNOWSHOES

Although the cross-country sled is designed for a one-man tow system, it works better on a team basis. With snowshoes, we use a trailing rope on the back of the sled which the second member of the team can use for braking a descent. Ordinarily, the lightly loaded team member breaks trail, the "mule" who tows the sled coming behind him. On a steep descent, however, the trail breaker waits for the mule to pass, grabs the trailing rope and follows downhill, anchoring at critical points. On an ascent, the trail breaker can double back to the foot of the slope and boost the sled from behind, either using his hands or placing the tip of his ski pole against the sled, taking care not to push the tip through the fabric cover. In steep, difficult terrain, the trail breaker may simply uncoil a section of rope as he moves upward, then anchor himself above. The mule then grips a loop at the end of the rope, lets his poles swing free, and with the assistance of his partner hauling from above, works his way up, pulling the sled.

The weight of the cross-country sled
shifts on different pitches.

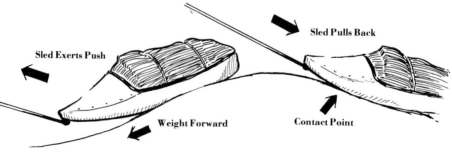

Sled Exerts Push

Weight Forward

Sled Pulls Back

Contact Point

2: *Packing in the Outfit*

THE CROSS–COUNTRY SLED WITH SKIS

Walking uphill on skis towing a sled behind is similar to uphill snowshoeing. On a gentle gradient, the skier can "walk up" just about the same way he would without the sled. On a steeper slope, he can herringbone his way up with some stout pole work. If the slope is too steep for that, teamwork is required, with one skier below pushing on the stern of the sled with the tip of his pole, the load going up a yard at a time. If this doesn't work, we simply take off our skis and walk the load up, one man in the harness, the other pushing from below.

Downhill skiing with a sled is something else. We have found no good way of roping down as a team. It is strictly a solo operation, but with several options: The skier can edge down or step down, using his poles for control; he can take off his skis and hike down, or he can figure out his route, shove off and ski down under control . . . or very nearly so. However, before making any extended winter trip with the sled, it pays to take out a loaded one and test its idiosyncrasies. It will have a few.

First, the sled does some funny things to a skier's turning. Turns must be anticipated earlier because the sled throws off the skier's timing. The weight of the sled pushes the skier ahead, and if he waits until he would normally make his turn, he may find himself off the trail and into the bush. Not only are turns started a little earlier if you are pulling a sled, but they must be made with more authority. When you are zipping down a timbered slope in the tracks of whoever is breaking trail, there is little opportunity to practice majestic Telemark turns. (In late winter on good crust and in open territory, such turns are possible.) Generally, it is a matter of following the tracks laid ahead, controlling your downhill speed with stems or poles, step-turning where necessary and trying to pick up a little extra momentum when a rise appears ahead.

Another phenomenon of downhill skiing with a cross-country sled is the push–pull factor. This is usually most evident at the foot of a slope rather than on the way down. On the downhill run, both skier and sled are clipping along at the same speed, almost as a unit, but at the bottom of the slope the situation changes. Few trails are absolutely flat, and when the skier goes over a bump or mogul, the sled catches lightly, pulling backward on his hips. This is no great disaster. It may merely yank the crouching skier upright. The problem arises when the sled comes off the downhill face of the bump and shoves the skier forward. It is often a very forceful shove, like being picked up bodily and hurled face-first into the snow.

The first time this happens, the skier invariably looks around from the place where he has been deposited, ready to chew somebody out for banging into him from behind. Some mental adjustment is required to accept the fact that it is simply the weight of the sled and Newton's Law of Gravity that caused the wipeout.

It takes a little practice to adjust to this pulling and pushing effect. With experience, the skier learns to "lean into" the harness as his feet go over a hump, then brace backward to take up the shove as the sled comes over. After a few spills, he will be reacting smoothly and automatically. By practicing with the loaded sled on an open slope, the skier can learn the few extra moves required. It is one thing to abort a downhill ski run on a twisting forest trail to avoid smacking into a tree. It is another thing to abort the run with a loaded sled behind—the sled may shove you into the tree anyway.

Care must be taken when encountering obstructions such as

stumps or rocks on a sharp turn. While the skier may easily negotiate the bend, the sled will take the shortest distance and may cut right across the obstacle, snagging on it. Possibly the only thing more surprising then having a sled shove you forward into the snow is to have it come to an abrupt halt, bending you at the hips so that your nose winds up against your ski bindings.

There is, of course, no reason for any mishap except carelessness and/or overconfidence. The skier must simply learn to operate a little differently with a sled in tow. To avoid fatigue, a team of two or three skiers should be used with a sled, changing off every half hour or hour between trail breaking and pulling the load.

Waxing for the Sled

A ski wax selected for an existing snow condition may be just right for maximum glide and swift climbing when the skier has no load other than himself. But with the addition of a sled and pack the situation changes radically, especially on the uphill climb. Because of the added weight and pull on the skier, his balance changes, and even with a more determined planting of his skis and poles he may find himself slipping backward. The tendency in this situation is to start slopping on soft wax, which may solve the uphill problem but creates some new ones on the flat or on the next downhill run when the goo turns the glide into a version of the hesitation waltz.

We don't have all the answers to this situation yet (well, name somebody who knows everything about waxing, anyway), but we have found that waxing as we would normally for the existing temperature is best at the start. Sometimes this works, sometimes not. If the skis start to slip we simply add a wax one color softer to the tips and tails and under the instep of the ski. This may do the job. If it doesn't, we wax the entire ski one color softer. For instance, if we started out with hard blue and a little purple kicker, we would go to hard purple with a little red kicker. Or maybe even purple klister if it was a warming day. Since nobody is keeping a stopwatch on this operation, there is time to experiment until the right combination is found. In times of doubt or disagreement, we have had several people wax differently—and then all of us use the combination that comes up best. It does not pay to keep struggling along on uphill slopes with the wrong wax. A muscle injury due to a slipping ski can be a real hangup miles from the end of the road.

Special Skis and Bindings

Most of us cannot afford more than one pair of cross-country skis at a time and we camp with whatever pair we own. However, it should be noted that the plastic-bottom "fish scales" or slotted skis work fine with the sled and present no wax problems. The reduced speed of these skis is not as big a factor when pulling a sled as when running without a load. If we could afford more than one pair of skis, we would probably have fish-scale bottoms for camping and our wooden smooth bottoms for cross-country day running. But then, maybe not. There are times on a crisp, hard-wax day when a long ride down a smooth, packed slope with the building momentum of a loaded sled is an exhilarating adventure. There is also satisfaction in picking out and applying the right wax combination. Even if foolproof, skidproof, nonwax, high-speed plastic bottoms were available, a lot of us would probably still use our old boards and wax.

Some experimenting is going on with varieties of plastic smooth-bottom skis in short lengths. The Canadian Armed Forces have developed a short winter ski, approximately 5 feet long and 4½ inches wide, which offers good support on deep snow. It is highly maneuverable and makes load pulling considerably easier. We have used these skis a few times and found them quite satisfac-

Ski bindings for heavy boots: A. Canadian type; B. Bentley type.

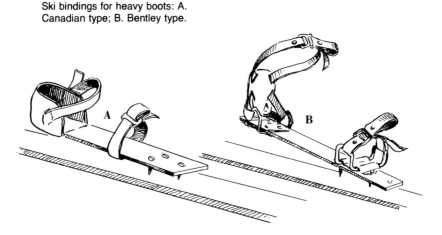

2: Packing in the Outfit

tory under heavy loads. They are equipped with a boot-type plastic binding featuring a single strap which allows the skier to operate with insulated pacs (those popular boots with leather uppers and rubber bottoms). In extreme cold, 30 below or lower, the insulated pac offers much less risk of frostbite than regular ski boots. With this type of binding, the skier needs only one set of boots on the trip. Some of the earlier bindings of this type were apt to break at the point of flex, but the new ones are tougher. They appear somewhat bulky but they do provide for good lateral movement and are a distinct plus on an extended trip when exposure to the cold is constant.

These Canadian bindings are not generally available to the public, but a good substitute is. Up at Tupper Lake, New York, Dick Bentley is testing and making an adjustable cold-weather boot binding called "Uni-Flex" which sells for around twenty dollars. It consists of a flexible plastic base with buckles and metal hinges which will allow almost any type of boot to be used comfortably. The binding fastens to the ski with three screws, giving almost the same freedom of movement as the pin bindings on most touring skis. The plastic base acts like the boot sole on a pin binding. Although the binding is a little bulkier and heavier than the ski boot–pin binding setup, it offers good lateral movement and allows the skier to wear a warmer boot.

3: Home in the Snow

A snug camp, a hot supper and a good night's rest after long hours on the trail not only restore body and soul but are essential to the campers' well-being and safety. The day plan calls for camp to be made well before dark, allowing adequate time for selecting and preparing the site, erecting the camp and gathering wood and water.

SELECTING THE SITE

The ideal winter campsite is a small, flat clearing in a wooded area, protected from the wind on all sides and adjacent to a good water supply. Where lakes and streams are pollution-free, a riffle or spring hole is handy and saves ice chopping. Snow is a safe source of water, but it requires some time to melt down because it is seventeen parts air to one part water. Campsites should be away from cliffs, ledges or steep inclines where drifting snow can build up and create slides.

Locating a sheltered tent site is not always easy. Most established campsites in the wild country of North America are situated for summer use in exposed locations, offering a breeze to keep the camp cool and free of bugs, and a scenic view of a lake, stream or valley. Wind-chill and drifting snow make these sites undesirable for cold-weather use, although there may be a sheltered location nearby. Moreover, established summer sites usually have a shortage of standing dead wood for making an open, warming campfire.

If, for some reason, a good sheltered site is not available, the tent should be pitched crosswind—that is, sideways to the available or anticipated prevailing wind. This placement will tend to eliminate most drifting and snow problems at the entryway. If the tent is placed back to the wind, the front door will drift shut. If it is front to the wind, snow will blow straight inside. It should be remembered that tents are designed to "spill" wind from the side, holding their rigidity. No matter how the tent is placed, however, exposed campsites do not insure a good night's sleep if the wind keeps the tent and fly clacking and snapping all night. Quiet, sheltered sites reduce flapping and are much better for sleeping, stove cooking and warming fires.

Advance Site Selection

The summer camper or guide who intends to visit the same general area in the winter may keep a sharp eye open for possible winter campsites, recording these in his journal or marking them on his map. Before the first snowfall, such sleep-wreckers as stumps, rocks and protruding roots are readily visible. When the ground is covered by a couple of feet of white fluff, it may be impossible to determine what is underneath without digging. Advance knowledge of good campsites can save a lot of extra hunting and digging when the party is tired and ready to camp.

Selecting a Site in Snow

Once a site is determined, we usually go over the entire area with our boots, kicking down to solid ground and then kicking and shuffling around to turn up any loose limbs or more permanent obstacles. If the site feels good to our feet, we are ready to clear it out.

When marking out the tent location, experienced campers look not only around, but also up. Snow-laden boughs of pine, fir or spruce should be shaken or poked clean so that a sudden wind does not cause a tent-flattening snow deposit during the night. The site is also checked for "widow makers," an old loggers' term for leaning dead trees or overhead dead limbs. Hardwoods, which have no leaves in the winter, sometimes appear to be dead. Loose bark and woodpecker holes will identify the really dead trees and branches.

PREPARING THE TENT SITE

Whenever it is physically possible, we shovel down to hard, bare ground. This reduces the amount of moisture beneath the tent floor and lowers the tent profile in the wind. All fallen limbs and other ground lumps are kicked loose and removed from the tent site. If there is a dip or hole, we may stamp that full of snow and

Clearing snow from tent site using an easily portable,
homemade plywood pack shovel.

pack it level. Better yet, we fill the low spots with slough grass or
brush tips to even it out. In no case do we use green material. Not
only is this poor camping practice but in many forests it is against
the law. The snow removed for the tent is piled up outside as a
wind-breaking wall, well away from the tent so that it does not
create a hole that will drift full overnight.

Where it is not feasible to dig down to earth, a serviceable platform can be tramped out with snowshoes or skis on the snow surface. Care is taken not to punch boot holes in the platform once it

3: *Home in the Snow*

is levelled and packed. With the molecular structure of the snow altered by packing, it will set up with a hard crust in about an hour and the tent can be pitched. The dug-out or stamped-out area should be several feet larger than the actual tent floor so that there is room to move around while putting up the shelter without kicking loose snow all over the fabric. At the entryway, a sizable area should be cleared off where boots and parkas can be shaken free of snow before the campers go inside. We usually make a small "deck" of wood poles, three to four inches thick, just outside the doorway where snow can be stamped off or brushed off with a whisk broom before entering the tent.

ERECTING THE TENT

When the tent is unrolled, the poles are left in the sled until actually needed. Nothing is taken out of a sled or pack and laid in the snow. There is an old saying, "Snow is the greatest thief in the North." Experience indicates that any items not specifically kept in a sled or pack will quickly vanish, swallowed up by the drifts.

With the tent stretched out on the site, the floor is staked out, the roof raised and walls guyed (unless you have one of the self-supporting type tents with an outside frame). Ordinary tent stakes do not work in snow or frozen ground. However, the tent sides may be lashed to poles laid parallel to the walls, the poles being held in place by snow piled on the ends. Anchors can be made from wooden discs or tree branches, tied on short lines to floor loops and buried in the snow. After the floor anchors are buried and the snow packed down on top of them, allow some time for the packed snow to "set up" before raising the roof or they will be pulled loose when the pole is pushed up.

With the floor anchored and the ridge raised, the tent walls and fly are guyed out, again using anchors made from branches, discs or even pieces of apple crate slats. Some camping supply houses stock excellent aluminum snow flukes which are worth looking into. Guy lines may also be lashed to poles sunk in the snow parallel to the tent or to nearby shrubs or saplings. When anchoring the tent you must consider what the situation will be when the camp is taken down. Dry snow stamped on top of a branch, disc or snow fluke will set up in a few minutes. It will hold a guy line solid and it breaks off easily when the tent is struck. If the snow is wet, however, as it is during a brief thaw, that packed snow will turn into balls of ice around the anchors. These must be broken away before the tent can be rolled up. In wet snow we sink the anchors only as deep as is required to hold the tent and we tie extra lines to nearby saplings or shrubs wherever possible.

Any snow which may have invaded the tent while it is being raised should be promptly swept out. A small whisk broom kept just inside the entryway is handy for cleaning the floor as well as brushing snow from clothing and boots. A wire hook held to the tent pole with a rubber band makes a handy hanger for the whisk broom.

TENT DESIGNS

Today's winter camper is fortunate in having a wide choice of excellent, lightweight tents manufactured expressly for tough weather. They are based on designs developed by high-country backpackers and explorers who required a warm shelter which would meet the tests of lightness, compactness, durability and ease of erection under extreme conditions. Many of these cold weather "expedition" tents will serve well for summer camping. However, few summer tents will qualify for winter use unless the owner modifies them expressly for that purpose.

Roofs

Winter tents require steeply pitched roofs to prevent snow build-up. Rain will run off any taut, waterproofed surface, even one with a very gradual slope. But a snowstorm hitting a poorly pitched roof can result in a rapid accumulation of weight, causing ropes to snap, ties to rip out, poles to bend and anchors to come loose, all of which may result in the tent collapsing on the occupants at a time when shelter is critical. Even with excellently designed tents, experienced campers make a practice of checking outside every few hours during a blizzard to make sure all guy ropes are tight and no snow is building up. It is cheap insurance.

Ease of Erection

When selecting a tent for winter use, it is a good idea to determine if a particular design can be put up almost entirely with mittens on. At 20, 30 or 40 below zero, bare hands do not perform intricate jobs with poles, fittings and knots. Also, the fewer pieces there are to a tent frame, the fewer there are to get lost in the snow.

Most winter tents come with sectional poles that telescope, break apart, or fold up for packing. Elastic cord connectors inside the poles work well as long as the pole sections are not allowed to snap forcibly in place and damage the connection. We pack our tent poles in a separate cloth bag so that pole tips or edges will not rub and damage the tent fabric on the trail. Guy ropes can all be tied with terminal loops before the trip starts so that no extra knots are necessary at the campsite. They can also be equipped with small plastic slides or adjusters for setting rope tension. These work on nylon rope up to $3/16$ inch and save a lot of time setting guy line tension. Some campers carry a half dozen or so short elastic cords with hooks on both ends to snap rope loops to anchors or saplings.

Tent Materials

"Breathable" synthetics such as ripstop nylon are currently the favored tent material. To work well, the tent weave must offer maximum protection against the wind while allowing air to circulate through the fabric. The only waterproof parts of the tent itself are the floors and short sidewalls. Covering the entire tent outside, however, is a lightweight, waterproof fly which is separated from the main tent by an air space. This keeps snow from piling up on the inner tent fabric and allows moisture originating inside to be carried off. To some extent the space between the tent and fly provides a layer of dead air insulation, as well.

Most "waterproof" tents simply don't work well in the winter. Fabrics treated to keep water out will also tend to keep moisture in. Each person gives off approximately one pint of water each night in the form of perspiration and condensed respiration. Some of this moisture escapes into the tent, and if it cannot flow readily through the fabric it will form a glaze on the interior. This may thaw and cause "rain" inside if a stove or lantern is lighted, making sleeping bags and clothing soggy and destroying their insulating value.

Breathable tents stop the wind but let moisture out where it will be deposited, if anywhere, on the fly. The fly can then be removed and shaken out. A frost liner may also be added inside the tent. This ties to the ridge and sides. It will capture much of the overnight moisture and can be removed each day and the ice crystals shaken or beaten out. Care must be taken when removing the frost liner not to shake ice crystals inside the tent.

Ventilation and Entrance Design

All good winter tents have adequate ventilation. Ventilation may be from a front door to back door or rear peak, or up through a tunnel vent in the tent vestibule. Good ventilation is necessary to carry off stove or lantern fumes, steam from cooking and human moisture.

In addition to ventilation, tent vestibules provide a place to remove boots and parkas without getting loose snow into the sleeping area. Good tents have tunnel entries through the vestibule or in both ends of the tent. These help keep snow and wind out. Double-tunnel tents can be connected to each other to conserve warmth and make inside cooking and socializing easier.

COOKING INSIDE THE TENT

While cooking should be done outside the tent as much as possible, there are some weather conditions in which cooking and eating inside is easier. All good winter shelters come equipped with a "cook hole" or "snow hole," a zippered flap in the tent floor or

Camp stove with pot in place, seated in the snow hole of a tent floor.

3: Home in the Snow

vestibule which can be laid back so that the stove rests on frozen earth or snow, not on the fabric. Fire is an ever-present hazard inside a tent, and extreme care must be taken with stoves, lanterns, candles, cigarettes and matches to keep the fabric from being ignited or scorched. There are flame-retardant fabrics—tent cloth chemically treated so that it will not flare up. But there is no such thing as a "fire-proof" tent fabric. They will all melt, char or burn in intense heat. Probably the greatest cause of tent fires is the flareup from a pressure stove lighted inside the tent. This can be caused by sloppy refueling, by overfilling the tank or by spraying fuel during the priming process. We always refuel stoves and lanterns outside, light them outside, and then bring them into the tent.

TENT SIZES

Tent size is a personal preference but there should be ample room for sleeping, eating if necessary, and storing some equipment. One advantage of the cross-country sled is that it allows one to carry larger tents. For two or three people, we prefer four-man shelters with six feet or so of headroom to allow standing up while dressing . . . or to remove a cramp in a leg muscle. The extra room also provides better air circulation. Some people, however, prefer small tents for their lightness and compactness. Some good four-man and two-man tents include:

Recreational Equipment, Inc. (REI), Mt. McKinley, 7½ by 8 feet, 7-foot 4-inch center height, single pole, 18-inch sidewalls, tunnel, cook hole and fly. Weight under 13 pounds. REI also makes a two-man Crestline Expedition model, with a 7-foot 4-inch-by-5-foot floor, 46-inch headroom, vestibule and cook hole, at about 10½ pounds with poles and fly (see Appendix I for addresses of these and other equipment outfitters).

Paul Petzoldt Wilderness Equipment has a Wand Tent, 8½ by 5 feet, with a steep roof with fiberglass stiffeners, 4 feet of headroom, two tunnels and a cook hole. It is very wind resistant for mountain use. It weighs about 12 pounds. Another model, the Petzoldt Expedition Shelter, is about the same size as the Wand, extremely tough in a wind, double tunnelled and equipped with a cook hole. Overall weight is about 11 pounds.

My own winter tent is an Alpine Design 8 by 8 foot model with

6 feet of headroom, single pole, steep roof, double entrance (one with tunnel), cook hole, ventilator, waterproof fly and optional flannel liner. This is very tough, well stitched at stress points and has given me years of service without any trouble. It doubles as a good spring and fall canoe camping tent.

Holubar markets a fine two-man Expedition Tent at 10 pounds, measuring 5 by 9½ feet, 47 inches at the ridge, with cook hole, tunnel, fly and frost liner, and easy-to-assemble outside pole suspension. Their four-person tent, which is simply named "Four Person Tent" is 8 by 8 feet, with a single pole, 6 feet at the ridge, double doored with a tunnel at the back. It rolls up into a tidy 10 pounds, 11 ounces.

North Face makes a roomy, four-man winter model called the Morning Glory, which has a hex-shaped floor with walls of an unusually steep, winged design. It has a large 14-by-8 foot floor with 6 feet of headroom. Its weight is under 13 pounds. The North Face St. Elias tent is a two-man model, 8 feet by 4 feet 8 inches, with frost liner and cook hole, and weighs in at about 9 pounds. A detachable vestibule is available that adds 42 inches to the tent length.

Gerry, one of the pioneers in lightweight backpacking, has several excellent winter or high-country tent models including the Himalayan, over 10 feet long with two vestibules, 5-foot width and 46-inches height at the ridge. It has a steep, reinforced roof, cook hole, tunnel entrance, frost liner and fly, all just under 13 pounds.

No good winter tent is cheap. You will not find them at bargain basement camping equipment sales. The cold-weather camper

Section diagram of snow shelter.

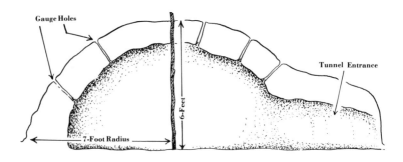

3: *Home in the Snow*

Snow houses on a winter camp site, northern Minnesota, 1978.

should recognize that he probably cannot get a good tent unless he is willing to pay from $180 to $300. However, the camper owning a quality A-frame summer tent with a sufficiently steep roof may convert his shelter to winter use with a little dexterity on the sewing machine. A vestibule can be designed and built with a tunnel, ventilator and snow hole. This can be attached to the front of the summer tent with tapes, a zipper or Velcro strips and simply removed and stored when summer comes. Materials for building a vestibule can be obtained from Frostline.

INSULATING THE FLOOR

Tent floors present twin problems of moisture and cold. If the floor is kept scrupulously swept of snow, moisture which could infiltrate sleeping bags or clothing can be reduced. If the floor is inspected from the inside against a light prior to the trip, tiny holes or scrapes can be detected and patched. If this is not done, snow melting under the tent can create moisture which will seep inside.

Whether the tent is pitched on frozen ground or on packed snow, it is much the same as camping on an ice cake. Cold continually comes through from below. Some campers use an extra tarp under the tent to reduce cold and prevent the tent floor from freezing to the ground. We use closed-cell foam inside, as we will explain in Chapter IV when we discuss sleeping gear.

SNOW SHELTERS

The Inuit built their permanent winter homes with driftwood or spruce pole frames packed with sod and moss, having walls eight inches thick or more. A seal oil stove in the middle of the house kept the temperature well above freezing and a hole in the roof carried away fumes and moisture. Sleeping was done on a raised platform covered with thick caribou hides.

The igloo was a temporary snow house built by the Inuit while on hunting trips. It was not used as a permanent shelter. Igloos are constructed spirally out of blocks about 30 by 18 by 18 inches, cut with a broad snow knife or machete, and bevelled so that each row slants inward to the center. If the igloo is built properly, the roof closes in with a single block filling the last hole in the ceiling. Loose snow is packed in the cracks and a stick is poked through the peak to make a ventilator. The entryway is a tunnel of blocks. Igloo construction requires a type of hard-packed snow which is seldom found in the forests of the Northland, but a fair substitute is sometimes found on open lakes where the wind can pack the snow, or in late winter when snow is freezing and thawing.

Easier to build than the igloo is a shelter carved out of a loose pile of snow. To begin construction, a pole is stuck up in the center of the site as a marker. Using a section of cord or rope, a circle is drawn around the pole in a radius of about seven feet. A dome-shaped pile of snow about 6 feet high is shoveled into the circle around the pole, with a smaller annex for an entryway. This is allowed to "set up" for an hour or so, then a tunnel is excavated through the annex and into the house, to the pole. This is best done by two men working together; one digs ahead, scooping the snow out, the other removes it from the tunnel to the outside. When the tunnel has been dug to the center pole, the interior radius of the shelter can be determined (usually a foot to 18 inches less than the outside radius) and a rope marked at that length and attached to the center pole to be used as a gauge. A bunch of sticks are poked about 18 inches into the roof from the outside to indicate to the excavator when he is approaching the right roof thickness. When the shelter has been completely dug out, the sticks are removed along with the center pole and the house is ready for occupancy.

For perhaps one day, heat can be used inside a snow house. After that a glaze forms and any heat much above freezing will result in dripping from the roof. However, a single plumber's candle will maintain a temperature inside of 10 to 15 degrees above zero, no matter how cold it may get outside, and a hardy camper can exist comfortably as long as he does not need extra heat for cooking or drying out clothing. Building snow houses can be very wet work, particularly when you are excavating the pile. Anyone planning to use a snow house for a campout should first make one in his back yard to determine how much energy is expended, how much time is required and how the drawbacks measure against the advantages of these shelters.

Some of the driftbusters we camp with prefer the snow house, and point out that all they need in the way of shelter equipment is a good shovel. And that may be. But I usually have my tent up, supper cooking and a warm fire drying out my pants long before they have moved into their accommodations. On the other hand, they do not have any problems breaking camp when it is time to head back. It is a matter of personal preference.

THE CAMPFIRE

We do very little cooking on a fire in the winter other than thawing out precooked meals packed in foil, but the fire is very important for warmth and for drying clothing. Getting a fire to burn in the winter can be a chore, depending on available fuel, wind and weather. It is no easier to start a fire in a blizzard than in a heavy rain. There is little point in memorizing various types of wood and which make the best fires . . . we simply use whatever dry wood is available. In the North this can be spruce, fir, aspen, birch, willow, alder, cedar, pine or any combination thereof.

Preparing the Site

We look for a flat spot, sheltered from the wind, and with no over-hanging branches which would catch fire or deposit a load of fire-quenching snow from laden boughs. Where possible, we dig down or kick down to bare rock or soil for our hearth. If we have to build the fire on top of snow, we pack the surface with our boots, lay out a platform of two-inch-thick sticks, and build the fire on this.

Gathering Fuel

Dry wood is essential, and this can be a fooler in the winter. Wood that appears dry may not be so inside. Generally, any branches found buried in the snow are worthless and will only smolder, at best. Leaning dead branches may or may not be dry, depending on how wet the last days of fall were before the freezeup. The best bet is to seek out standing dead saplings in thick woods and knock them over or cut them off. For tinder, the outer bark from dead birch, dry weed stalks and the lower, dry branches from spruce, fir or pine are excellent. For the sake of leaving a clean, untouched site, we do not remove any lower dead limbs from trees close to our campsites.

Fire Starting

Jack London once wrote an absorbing tale of a man who died in the Yukon because he failed to lay his fire properly and fumbled away all his matches with numb hands. When the moment arrives to pull off our mittens and strike the match, we want that fire to ignite without delay. There are a couple of ways to insure instant fire:

One is the use GI surplus Hexamine tablets or some other type of fire starter tabs which will catch immediately and burn hot even in the snow. Another way is to use a ball of ordinary wax paper as tinder. We do not use stove fuel to start a fire. It can be done, but it is a bad habit and a good many campers have been broiled or blown into orbit using it.

We use a dry three-inch-thick chunk of wood for a "back log," lay our fire tablet or wax paper against it and then prop layers of small twigs or weed stalks against the back log over the tinder, following up with some half-inch sticks. The match is struck and

3: Home in the Snow

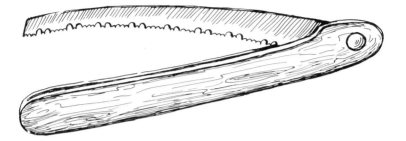

Folding firewood saw.

additional twigs and sticks are added until the fire will handle larger material.

Maintaining the Fire

It takes an unbelievable supply of wood to keep a fire operating, and since many camping areas are getting short of wood, efficient use of fuel is essential. Warming and drying should be done, insofar as possible, by everyone at one time, then the fire should be allowed to go out.

We use a small folding saw to buck up firewood. It is much lighter and safer than an axe. There are several additional problems presented by an axe on a winter trip. First, the blade must be kept sheathed when not in use and there is something about an axe sheath that makes it want to hide in a snowdrift. Second, an axe can be downright dangerous in cold weather when hands are numb or mittens get slippery with ice. Not only can the chopper injure himself with a deflected blow, but the handle can slip and the axe sail halfway across the campsite. Some campers take an axe along to chop water holes in the ice, but this is not nearly as satisfactory as a good ice chisel, and can be impossible when the ice is three feet or more thick. There are some top-notch campers who would rather be caught without their boots than without their axe, and they are skillful choppers. But I have never seen an axe buck up wood any faster than a good camp saw.

Fire-Building   31

Winter camp biffy.

THE BIFFY

Essential to the comfort and welfare of any camp is the location and construction of a good outdoor toilet. Ideally, we seek a sheltered nook in the underbrush, close to camp yet providing a modicum of privacy. Two trees about ten inches in diameter and three to four feet apart make a sturdy base. We kick down in the snow between the trees and then remove any leaves, twigs or moss that can be set to one side. These will be used to cover the site when camp is abandoned.

Two smooth, sturdy poles about three inches in diameter are lashed between the trees, on opposite sides. The lower one is adjusted for height to make a seat, the upper one used as a backrest. Skilled biffy-builders are not easy to come by, and when one is discovered who can speedily lash up a good facility, he is awarded an honored place in the group. Some campers leave a roll of paper

3: *Home in the Snow*

at the biffy, stuffed inside an empty two-pound coffee can or some other shelter, but we don't. Squirrels have a habit of gnawing holes in toilet paper with dismaying results. We keep our paper bagged in plastic at the campsite, taking a roll out to the biffy as needed.

When breaking camp, we untie the poles, remove the rope, cover the site between the trees with the duff and moss removed earlier and then sprinkle over a covering of snow. Some meticulous campers take their used paper back to the camp and burn it in the fire. Some put a match to it right at the biffy. Some do not even carry paper but use a handful of snow instead. Although human wastes disintegrate rapidly through bacterial and plant activity once warm weather comes, toilet paper does not degrade as fast, although it will eventually. We are concerned mainly that it is anchored down and does not get blown about the campsite. If it isn't burned, a layer of turf and twigs under the snow cover will usually handle the problem.

4: Winter Sleeping Gear

Nowhere in the camping equipment revolution have changes been more dramatic than in the development of warm, lightweight sleeping systems. Greatest impetus came during World War II when thousands of servicemen discovered the advantages of the down-and-feather GI mummy bag. Crude by today's standards, the U.S. Army sleeping bags "leaked" duck feathers through the fabric, but they were light, easily packed, had a tough functional zipper and when kept dry, offered a fair barrier against Europe's winter chill. Such additions as a foam pad underneath were unknown and there was plenty of heat transfer between cold ground and human bodies, but the bags still beat blankets by a mile. As GI surplus after the war they filled a void until manufacturers began turning out the superb bags we now take for granted. As a good many of us oldsters who did their first snow camping with wool blankets can testify, right now are the "good old days" of winter camping.

Today's camper has it so good because he is witnessing a battle for the market which pits down against synthetic fiber and one style of quilting against another, and is heightened by controversy over cover materials, zippers and shapes as well as various types and lengths of foam pads. All of this means warmer, more economical equipment. This is not to imply that good equipment is cheap. It isn't. Nor that there is no schlock sleeping gear being foisted on the unwary, because there is. For those who do not have their sleeping gear selected or who may be contemplating colder situations, an examination of what is available may be in order.

SLEEPING BAGS

The modern bag consists of two fine-weave, lightweight shells filled with compartments of insulation. Its aim is to keep as much body heat as possible trapped inside the bag while as much body moisture as possible is allowed to seep out. The body manufactures the heat, the bag doesn't. Trapping that heat is what design, fill and materials are all about.

Cover Materials

Almost all the bags sold for cold-weather camping have "ripstop nylon" shells. Ripstop nylon is a tough, light, high-density synthetic DuPont fabric which resists moisture, yet allows air to pass through. It comes in several weights, ranging from 1.2-ounce to 1.9-ounce. The best winter bags in terms of strength and density are made from 1.9-ounce ripstop nylon. When used in conjunction with down this material tends to "leak" less. Nylon taffeta is also used, mainly as interior liner material in less expensive bags.

Fill

Fill is the bag's insulating material, the stuff that provides the minute dead air spaces which trap the heat. Modern winter bags are made of goose down, Polarguard, Dacron II or Holofil II. There are an awful lot of claims and counterclaims being made about these fill materials, and what is going to be printed here may annoy some people.

First, let's take a look at down, which is the soft, dense insulating undercover that keeps waterfowl warm and comfortable. There are a lot of differences in downs. Duck down is neither as durable nor as effective in heat retention as goose down. There are also some great variations in goose down. Bag and clothing makers are becoming more critical about down quality. Most goose down comes from Asia and northern Europe. It's costly, and in the past some suppliers diluted the imported material with extra feathers or reclaimed used down, lessening its insulating properties. While there is still some chiseling going on, bag labels listing the fill as "Prime Northern Goose Down" usually indicate quality fiber.

The chief advantages of down are its "loft" or fluffiness, its high insulation quality in proportion to its weight and its compressibility. Its chief disadvantage is its tendency to soak up and retain moisture. There have been a lot of tests conducted which show that goose down has heat-retaining qualities superior to those of synthetic fibers, but these tests do not tell the whole story.

Let's take a look at what happens to down under normal winter camping conditions. As noted before, the human body gives off a pint of moisture during a night's sleep. Some of this moisture escapes into the tent as you breathe, but the rest has to filter through the sleeping bag. While the inside layer of the bag, near the body, stays warm, the fill gradually cools as you approach the outside cover, which is the same temperature as the air in the tent. As the escaping body moisture drifts up through the down it reaches the dew point and condenses. It is a small quantity the first night and does not noticeably affect either the warmth or the weight of the bag. But the next night, the same thing occurs. By the end of the week, the bag is getting heavy and is stiff to unroll. It is also rapidly losing its heat-retaining properties. The tiny down filaments are getting soaked and frozen. And they do not release their moisture. Neither sun nor wind nor a wood fire will get that moisture out of the filament. On an extended trip, that down bag may easily turn from a source of comfort to a frigid trap.

Frankly, I like down. My wife and I have two fine goose down bags which we use for short winter trips, up to five days. But on longer trips we would consider nothing except synthetics. It is just too risky. Furthermore, the average winter traveller who sometimes crawls into his bag with wet socks or damp underclothes will be adding to his problems in a down bag. A fully wet down bag is no more useful than a sack of frozen oatmeal, and there is no way to dry it out in the bush. Even back in civilization, a down bag can be thoroughly dried only in a commercial drier. Hanging it in the house to dry takes forever. Realistically, we consider the down bag to be good only on short winter trips if care is taken to keep it meticulously dry. So what about synthetics?

Synthetic Fiber

Among the three materials currently available for winter bags— Polarguard, Dacron II and Holofil II—we can detect no difference in insulation qualities. Polarguard is a continuous-filament Celanese fiber which comes in a mat that is easy to handle if you are making bags or garments. Dacron II and Holofil II are DuPont products that come in shorter, slippery fibers that shift around and are not easy for the do-it-yourself bag or parka maker to handle. Commercial manufacturers have no trouble with any of these fillers.

What is the advantage of synthetic fill? Mainly, it has to do with moisture. Neither Polarguard nor the Dupont products will absorb moisture. While moisture may get inside the bag, it isn't soaked up. It tends to migrate to the cover where it can be beaten off the surface or dried out by the sun or by a fire. And since water does

4: Winter Sleeping Gear

not affect the fibers, they still offer good insulation even if the bag gets damp. The bag can be dried by turning it inside out (since the inside lining shell is thinner material than the outside it releases moisture more quickly) and hanging it in the sun and wind. Even on a bitter cold day the moisture will be released. Or it can be dried by heat from the fire. Some pretty reputable people in the outdoors, like Paul Petzoldt of the National Outdoor Leadership School, make no bones about the advantage of synthetic fibers over down when it comes to the problem of moisture. Their views are based on extensive use under tough winter conditions.

Why doesn't everybody use synthetics? They have disadvantages, too, the main one being that they do not compress as well as down and are therefore bulkier. A synthetic-fill bag is also somewhat heavier than a down bag with the same insulating value. Bag makers tell us that the chemical companies are working on weight and compressibility and that new synthetics are anticipated which will have those properties of down and yet stay moisture free. But right now we have to use what is available.

Combination Bags

Winter campers, being naturally inquisitive and seldom satisfied with a status quo, have come up with the idea of a synthetic fiber bag with a separate inside down liner. This would seem to be getting back to the moisture problem, but that isn't how it works. Apparently the body moisture filters through the down liner and, because the liner is warm throughout, does not begin to condense until it gets into the synthetic outside shell where it is not a problem. With this type of combination bag, compressibility and lightness are possible, insulation is insured and moisture reduced. Such bags were used by the 1977 Ellesmere Island Expedition for fifty-two days without difficulty. Other tests by winter campers show similar results. For campers who can afford them, these bags appear to be the best bet right now.

There is another advantage of the combination bag which is readily apparent: The camper can remove the down liner and use the synthetic bag in the summer. Double bags are nothing new, of course—manufacturers have been making double synthetic bags for year-round use for some time. But it is just recently that the synthetic–down double bag has begun to appear . . . or that anybody has understood why it really works in extreme cold.

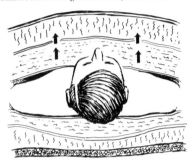

Body moisture trapped in down sleeping bag (left) is less a problem in down-synthetic combination bag.

The camper who already owns a good Polarguard or Holofil II spring-to-fall bag can purchase a lightweight goose down liner and equip himself with a winter bag . . . that is, if his synthetic bag is big enough and comes equipped with a good hood. Or, if he owns a hooded down bag, he can buy a large-size synthetic fiber bag for his outside shell. Years ago, before we could afford a good winter bag, we got by with stuffing one three-pound Dacron II bag inside another one borrowed from a friend. It was pretty bulky to roll up, but it was warm enough.

About here someone will say: "How come you don't use double Polarguard bags?" And we do. The double Polarguard, the outside bag slightly larger than the inside, works just about as well as the down-and-Polarguard bag. It is just a little bulkier and heavier.

CONSTRUCTION

Insulation inside a sleeping bag is held in place by fabric walls stitched between the inner and outer shells. This construction is necessary to keep the fibers from shifting around and leaving some areas with no insulation. Cheap summer bags are quilted with a simple stitching straight through the material which allows for little insulation where the seam occurs. Winter bags are built with baffles inside like boxes—square, slanted, "V" shaped or laminated—so that the insulation continually overlaps leaving no cold spots. In good bags, the inner shell is made slightly smaller than the outer shell—a process termed "differential cut"—so that the

4: *Winter Sleeping Gear*

loft of the fill is uniform between the layers. In the best bags, the seams are double stitched around the hood and at places of stress such as alongside the zipper. If you do not know what double stitching is, take your mother along when you buy a bag and let her take a close look at the work. In some cases, we have simply restitched an otherwise good bag, going over the stress points a second time. All of this designing, cutting and sewing requires extra operations from skilled labor which add to the cost, but also to the quality.

One area of sleeping bag construction which needs some good research is a comparison of the moisture-releasing properties of the various types of baffles. While body moisture can drift up through the dead air space in the fill, any wall of cold nylon cloth tends to stop it and condense it. The testing we have done, admittedly not very scientific, has made us suspect that when the baffle walls are vertical between the inner and outer shell, moisture is more easily released. But this is just a guess from field observations. It would be a service to cold-weather campers if some of the manufacturers would run moisture tests on the various types of baffle construction. They might even come up with a whole new concept in moisture release.

Fasteners

Most good winter bags come with big #10 Ykk Delrin zippers which do not tend to frost up and stick in the cold. The best bags also have an insulated tube or flap which runs parallel to the zipper on the inside, sealing the zipper opening off from outside drafts. Some bags have a full-length zipper, others have one only halfway down the side. The better full-length types can be opened from either the top or bottom, an advantage on a warm night when less heat needs to be trapped. However, the choice of zipper is mainly a personal one.

All good winter bags have zipper tabs inside as well as outside. If the inside tab is gripped in such a way that the thumb moves ahead of the slide, the liner material will be pushed away from the zipper teeth as the bag is opened or closed. About the only time the fabric will get caught in the zipper is when somebody is in one heck of a hurry to get his bag zipped up. When the cloth gets caught and the zipper jammed, he may start to yank on the liner instead of patiently reversing the zipper and easing the material away from the teeth. Once the material acquires a rip it is infinitely easier to get it caught in the zipper teeth again. Such spots should be promptly repaired.

Designs

There are three principal bag styles: square, tapered and mummy. Square bags offer a maximum amount of room, particularly for the feet, but they also have a lot of waste space resulting in extra weight and bulk. Few winter bags are cut square any more except those made on special order for a few diehards who get claustrophobia in a closer fitting bag. Tapered bags eliminate waste space and still provide a certain amount of looseness. Mummy bags are just that: a cocoon.

For winter use we prefer either the tapered bag or a slightly oversized mummy bag. There is little difference in their weight and bulk. Either offers enough room inside to allow the camper to add more clothing on an extremely cold night. All winter bags are equipped with hoods which can be closed around the face, leaving only the nose and mouth exposed. If the camper puts his entire face inside the bag, he will create a wet spot where his breath condenses.

TOGETHERNESS

In some sleeping bag advertisements, one occasionally comes across an illustration showing the side-by-side, zipped-together sleeping bag arrangement. While this may have some romantic appeal, it is a bummer for winter work. There is no really good way to seal two bags together and chilly drafts will slip down the gap. Furthermore, when one person turns over in the bag, he moves the whole bed, waking his companion. Zipped together bags may be great for watching a football game in a cold stadium, but they aren't very practical for a sub-zero night's sleep.

HALF BAGS

There are some military units and a few hardy recreational campers who carry the "shorty" bags—small, compact, lightweight sleeping robes that come just above the waist—and use their parkas to

40

cover the upper half of their bodies. This method is used by some Scandinavian arctic troops, and they function quite well. They also pack almost twice as many men inside a tent as would normally sleep together on a recreational venture, the packed bodies providing a considerable amount of heat in themselves. While there is some merit in saving weight and reducing the amount of equipment, it should be kept in mind that people born and raised in the far north readily adapt to situations which most of us would consider uncomfortable at best. Unless the camper is quite acclimated to sleeping in sub-zero conditions, it is doubtful that he will be comfortable in a half bag.

MATS

It takes only an hour or so for the warm-weather camper with his summer bag and air mat to discover that such a system will not work in the winter . . . even if he can get the air mat unrolled and blown up. Having that cold air cushion under the compressed part of your sleeping bag is not conducive to comfort. Foam, so far, has been the best answer.

The two most popular types of mats now in use are 2 inch thick polyurethane (open cell) foam and ³/₈ to ½ inch thick polyethylene, unicellular (closed cell) foam. For cold weather work we have found the unicellular foam best since it offers the most protection from the frozen ground and does not absorb moisture. Open-cell mats are softer and compress better, but they do not protect as well and have a bad habit of creating puddles between the bag and the tent floor. We prefer full-length closed-cell pads which insulate the entire body, including the legs, from the frozen ground. One of the best-known closed-cell brands is Ensolite. It is available from any backpacker supply house.

It takes some getting used to the fact that not only the cold air above the tent can cause discomfort, but also the frozen ground or snow below. Without good insulation against the ground or snow, the heat transferred from the body will begin thawing out pockets where the hips, buttocks and shoulders hit, creating depressions which will collect moisture. During the last couple of winters we have used somewhat oversized closed-cell mats, three of which will cover the entire floor of the tent, insulating the shelter completely from the ice and snow beneath. While this adds a little more bulk to our outfit, it adds a lot more comfort to the tent.

There is another reason that floor insulation is important, other than personal comfort. Moisture which forms beneath the floor will turn to ice, forming unwieldy chunks that may be difficult to break off when rolling up the tent. Or the ice may "cement" the tent to the ground underneath, a frustrating development when the group is eager to break camp and be on the trail. If this occurs, the tent floor must be raised carefully, the ice knocked loose a little at a time and attention given to making sure that the floor material and waterproof coating are not cracked or ripped.

SLEEPING COMFORTABLY

Sleeping bags are usually rated as to Fahrenheit temperature range on charts showing 25 degrees, 15 degrees, zero, −20 degrees and so forth. While this may give some indication of a bag's insulating value, it only reveals part of the story. In an exposed, windy location, the insulation value will lessen considerably. This is why we camp in tents and not out in the open. Also, the warmth of a bag can be altered considerably by what is worn in it. Few winter campers go to bed in the buff, at least not twice in their lives. While it may sound ridiculous, a good number of frostbite cases have resulted from people sliding their bare feet across the cold nylon lining of a frigid bag. This can occur quite easily because the feet may be cold already and partially numb. People who attempt to slide a bare posterior into a cold nylon bag will seldom get farther than the initial contact.

There are a wide variety of sleeping clothes preferences. I like a suit of quilted dacron underwear, combined with a pair of dry socks, dacron boot liners (if it is very cold) and a knit cap for my head. In the early part of the night, while the tent is still relatively warm and I may have my head outside the bag for reading as well as sleeping, the knit cap keeps my skull from getting cold. Later, as the cold settles in with more authority, I pull my head inside the hood and the cap keeps me comfortable while the nylon liner warms up. Then I pull the cap off. If some emergency arises during the night, the quilted underwear, cap, boot liners and socks help retain warmth while I climb into pants, boots and parka.

In any event, we do not normally wear our day travel clothing to bed. Pants, shirts, socks and mitten liners which did not get thoroughly dried out before bedtime, will pretty well dry out inside the sleeping bag if they are spread out flat along the sides. Parkas are usually rolled up in the sleeping bag stuff sack and used for pillows.

CARE OF SLEEPING GEAR

It is absolutely essential to keep sleeping gear free of snow, ice, dampness and dirt. The entire insulation program depends on this. Too often we have seen the results when a weary camper climbed into a down bag, feet numbed or edging into frostbite, and the bottom of the bag was iced up from snow or wet socks. Unless that camper has some alert and knowledgeable companions along, he is a first-class candidate for frostbite. At worst an icy bag is a good invitation to hypothermia.* At best it is doggone uncomfortable and prevents needed slumber.

Every bit of snow is kept out of the tent and away from the bags. Completely. If not taken care of, snow can cause real problems. It is simply not possible to dry even the best synthetic bag inside the tent. It must be taken outside. In dry, sunny weather, a bag hung over a line inside out will dry even when the temperature is far below zero. But it is not always possible to arrange dry sunny weather in advance. Sometimes it snows for days on end.

Hanging a bag out in the snow is worse than not hanging it at all. That is why we haul an extra tarp and extra rope in the sled. A tarp slung high off the ground offers a good shelter under which to dry out bags, mats and wet clothes. In some situations when the snow was compact, we have used our snow knife to cut blocks, arranged these to form a wall on the windward side, slung the tarp overhead and built a fire in front. This provided a fair drying situation. If we can't cut blocks, we shovel the snow into a windbreak, sometimes using dead brush or blowdowns to form the inside wall. But any way it is done, the sleeping gear must be kept dry.

IT WAS NO FUN FOR THE EXPLORERS

The problem of moisture in sleeping gear or in clothing is no recent phenomenon. Some of the best educational reading on winter

---

* This is a serious condition in which heat loss from the body results in a temperature drop from which the body cannot recover by itself. It is discussed in detail in Chapter X.

camping is available in the journals of arctic explorers in the 1800's and early 1900's. Many members of these expeditions came to grief, not from the cold, but from dampness. In every instance, the expedition began with the men warm and well insulated against the climate, both in clothing and sleeping gear, but as the days wore on, moisture gathered in their garments and bedding, reducing their value until the men were wearing stiff, ice-encased parkas and had to almost break their bedding apart to get in it. The drain on their energy required for their bodies to maintain warmth in this situation, coupled with the rigors of trail travel, destroyed them. Arctic travellers like Vilhjalmur Stefansson, who spent years living with the Inuit, adopted the trouble-free native method of using caribou skins, which provided excellent insulation and allowed the moisture to be carried off. Fortunately for us, the Celanese and Dupont laboratories have made it possible for today's camper to exist comfortably in sub-zero temperatures without making any further demands on the remaining caribou herds.

CARE AFTER THE TRIP

While moisture is the most immediate hazard on a winter trip, accumulated dirt can also cause a loss of insulation and ventilation. Dirt collects inside a bag as well as out. As noted before, anything which prevents the free flow of moisture from inside the bag to the outside will cause that moisture to condense and build up inside, destroying insulating quality. A dirty bag is an invitation to frostbite. While it may not appear that there is any visible "dirt" blowing around in the winter, body oils will build up inside a bag and small particles of sand, leaves and bits of food will infiltrate the outer cover during continual use. Periodically, this dirt should be removed. Most bags now made, both down and synthetic fiber, can be washed with a little care. Instructions for cleaning a bag are usually included in a little folder or tag that comes with the product. Almost any bag can be hand washed in lukewarm water in a large laundry tub or bathtub. A non-detergent soap such as Ivory or Woolite will not harm the fibers. The bag is pushed and kneaded to work out the dirt, not twisted, since this can rip the baffles. When the bag has been thoroughly worked with soap, it is rinsed several times in lukewarm water until the suds vanish. The water is drained off the bag, then the bag is pressed against the tub until all possible excess water is squeezed out. This lightens the bag so that it will not be damaged when it is picked up (such damage is much less likely with synthetic fibers than with down).

Down bags dry best when tumbled dry in one of the large driers at a laundromat . . . set at warm, not hot. Hanging it on a line can take a long time and tends to make the down bunch in pockets. Synthetic bags can be tumbled dry or hung up. Since the fill does not absorb water, these bags dry out relatively quickly. When dry, really dry, the bag should be rolled up loosely and stored on a shelf. It is jammed into the stuff bag only when being packed for a trip.

Before the clean bag is put away for storage, it should be gone over carefully, the fabric and stitching examined to reveal any holes or pulled threads. If baffle stitches come loose, a wall may collapse and the fill may shift, piling up in one place and leaving little except two layers of thin ripstop nylon somewhere else. Repairs can be made by hand or by a good seamstress, but they should be done at the first sign of damage. Once a large length of seam is gone, it is almost impossible to restore a baffle without ripping that section of the bag apart and removing the fill.

The most common problems that occur in bags are cigarette burn holes, "melted" segments of the outer cover where somebody carelessly set a hot cook pot, or shredded pieces of inner liner that got caught in the zipper. Holes can be patched by hand. The patches may not look pretty but they will keep the fill from leaking out. Rips caused by zippers are usually near the zipper seam and can be cross-stitched on a machine.

Foam mats can be swept off and shaken to remove dirt. They can also be washed in lukewarm water, rinsed and dried.

5: Clothing for Winter Camping

In the choice of apparel for winter camping, the latitude is quite wide, as is quickly proven by observing large groups of cross-country skiers or snowshoe travellers. While there is no set uniform for winter camping, there is a great difference in individuals' tolerance of cold, and there are some designs and materials which protect better than others.

The camper needs two sets of wearing apparel (which may overlap considerably)—one set to use while in motion on the trail and the other set for the less active life in camp.

OUTFITS FOR TRAVEL

Not everybody's heat production is the same, and therefore each person has to work out his own clothing system. The friends with whom I camp and ice fish consider me a little weird because I am generally dressed fairly lightly. This may be because my heat machine pumps out a lot of BTU's, or it may be that I just feel better being cool. I do not, on the other hand, have a good tolerance to heat, which is probably why I live in the north country instead of the tropics.

The best system devised for keeping the body comfortable in the winter has been to dress in a number of layers of clothing. These layers trap the body heat by providing insulating dead air spaces and they also have the advantage of being removable, one at a time, so that the amount of insulation can be adjusted to conform to the amount of heat being produced by the body.

There has been enough information written on the subject of layering so that it would seem that everyone going outdoors in the winter should have this concept firmly in mind. But we still meet people on the trails puffing along, red-faced and dripping with perspiration because they are wrapped tight in a huge parka and encased in quilted, down-filled pants. On one-day tours this is usually no disaster, since the trip will terminate in a heated lodge or a heated car and a quick ride home. But when home is a tent and the night chill is creaking down hard and unforgiving, nobody should be caught with his teeth chattering in wet clothes. Let's take a look at a good layering system, from the skin out.

Next to the Skin

We start our layers with lightweight, thermal net long johns, which allow moisture to escape while retaining considerable heat. These are the "fishnet" underwear suits that have huge holes that look like they would leak all the body heat away. In fact, they hold warmth by creating dead air space in the openings of the net. Because this underwear is next to the skin, it is right up against the source of moisture as well. Therefore, the good suits are made out of fifty percent polyester, which will not absorb water, and fifty percent cotton for softness. Cotton by itself is not a very good insulator. When cotton gets wet it draws heat from the body as a lamp wick draws oil. Wool, of course, retains much of its insulating properties even when wet, but plain wool itches. Some campers prefer the Duofold type underwear to the fishnet because it has a cotton inner lining that wicks away the perspiration and a wool, cotton and nylon outer layer that retains the heat. So far, the fishnet and Duofold are the best we have tested.

For our foot covering, next to the skin, we use socks that are seventy to eighty percent wool mixed with synthetic fiber for smoothness and durability. Worsted wool socks are less scratchy, but they are not as durable as wool and synthetic. The only problem with wool is that it soaks up perspiration. It maintains its insulating qualities, but it gets wet. Therefore, the feet get wet inside the boots. To get away from that problem, some snow travellers wear light Dacron socks inside the wool ones. The foot's moisture goes through the Dacron and collects in the wool, but since the Dacron stays dry the foot remains relatively dry.

Middle Layer

Over the undergarments, from the bottom up, goes our second layer of insulation. If it is a very cold day and we are on skis, this

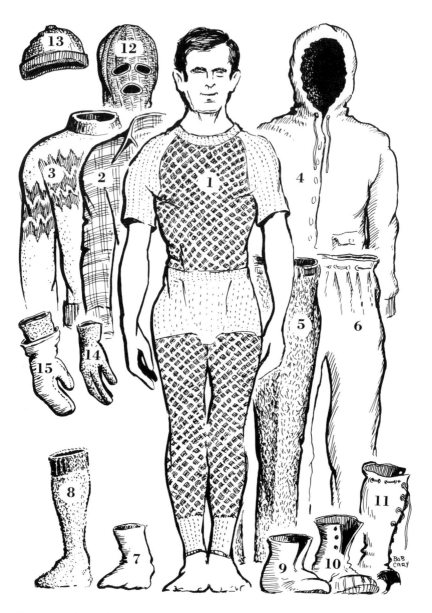

Dressing in layers for warmth: 1. Net underwear; 2. Wool shirt; 3. Sweater; 4. Wind parka; 5. Wool pants; 6. Outer wind pants; 7. Dacron sock; 8. Outer wool sock; 9. Boot liner; 10. Boot; 11. Gaiter; 12. Face mask; 13. Wool hat; 14. Wool gloves; 15. Mitt with liner.

may mean a second pair of wool socks inside our pin binding boots. If we are using bigger boots such as Sorels for snowshoeing, we may put on quilted Polarguard boot liners. In bitter cold we may wear loose, quilted Dacron underwear pants and then wool pants. If it is an ordinary zero or above-zero winter day, the wool pants can go right over the Duofold or fishnet. Most veteran skiers advocate suspenders to hold the pants up rather than a belt because the belt constricts the waist. However, some of us wear belts anyway, just out of hardheadedness.

Over the underwear, above the belt, we wear a wool shirt. On extremely cold days we put the upper half of the quilted Dacron underwear over the shirt, not under it. The reason for this is that if we have to layer back, it is easier to take off the quilted jacket if it is over the shirt.

Outside Shell

It is the job of the outside layer to keep the dead air from shifting underneath or at least to control that movement. The outside, from the bottom up, consists of boots, gaiters, light but closely-woven wind pants (we use GI wind pants which are somewhat baggy but tuck in at the ankles and waist), a sweater, wind parka, headgear and mittens.

A loose-knit sweater provides additional warmth around the heart and lungs as well as the arms and is an easily removable layer. On a still, warm day we may remove the wind parka and travel only in the sweater. It is a very old European system but it is still one of the best.

The wind parka is a finely woven, unlined, loose-fitting garment with a hood. Its job is simply to act as a shell. We like the type with a low, tie-down skirt, a waist cord and wrist closures. The once common wolf fur face ruff is now mostly fictional because there are not that many timber wolves any more. Some wind parkas come equipped with adjustable, wire-reinforced hoods that create a long tunnel of dead air leading to the face. While these may be the ticket for arctic work or windy high-country travel, they are not necessary for ordinary winter treks through the forests. We use a hood that just snugs in around the face.

In very cold weather we sometimes use a down vest under the wind parka or even start out with a down or Polarguard parka as our outer garment. Usually, however, these are too warm for travelling and we keep them in the duffle for less active camp life. These fluffy parkas can be zipped open to emit excess heat but they are not handy flapping around a backpack or sled harness.

Mittens and Gloves

In moderate winter conditions, insulated ski gloves may keep the hands warm, but we have found that layered mittens work better. We start with wool GI knit gloves covered by knit inner mitts and soft, supple, outside leather mittens, preferably deerskin. The inner knit gloves allow the traveller to take off his mitts to adjust straps or harnesses without exposing his bare skin to the cold. It also saves a lot of grief when handling objects such as buckles, chisels, stoves or tent poles in sub-zero weather, when severe frostbite "burns" will occur if metal comes in contact with the skin. The outside leather mitten and wool liner can be slipped on quickly when the chore is completed or if the fingers begin to stiffen. Layering off in warmer weather, we simply pull out the knit mittens and stuff them in our pack.

SPECIAL NOTES ON FOOTGEAR

The feet present a problem in winter travel that has not yet been solved. We have some passable systems, but there are probably more serious frostbite cases involving the feet than any other part of the anatomy. There is an old saying: "Keep your head and feet warm and the body will be warm." This is pretty close to the truth. The feet are the extremity farthest from the heart, have the poorest circulation and sweat a lot, all of which make them more susceptible to cold.

Boots should always be a little loose because tight boots cut circulation. Loose boots also allow for layering inside the boot. When we are on snowshoes, we generally use the rubber-bottom pacs with gaiters, but in some dry cold situations we have found that mukluks or high-top Indian moccasins work better because they are less likely to retain moisture inside.

Any of these boots is only as good as its liner and most commercial liners are made of felt. Felt is cheap and is a fair insulator as long as it is dry, but on the trail it tends to absorb moisture and become soggy. If those damp felt liners are not taken out of the

Winter moccasin boot in snowshoe
with insole and insulated liner.

boot and dried at night, the boot will be a chunk of ice in the
morning and impossible to put on. This happens often and it is not
funny. We have found two types of liners which work much
better—Finlander tossus and Polarguard booties. Tossus are made
of raw wool, soaked in water and beaten by hand into shape around
a foot form. In northern communities where there is a thriving
Finnish population, these liners can be purchased, but they are
not common elsewhere. Under trail conditions they easily dry out,
retain their fluffiness and wear better than felt. They can be tucked
inside the sleeping bag at night and dried out that way.

We make our own boot liners with inner and outer Dacron
shells enclosing a Polarguard batt. Since the Polarguard will not
absorb moisture, the perspiration from the feet travels through the
socks and the liner and winds up on the outside of the liner. The
feet and socks stay warm and relatively dry, and the Polarguard
liner can easily be taken out of the boot and dried. For extreme
cold, from minus 30 to 50 degrees, we use three sets of Polarguard
liners in each boot. The first liner fits the foot, while the second
and third are each slightly larger to allow for maximum insulation
without constricting the foot. Obviously, such a setup calls for a
slightly oversized boot. For a proper fit, we wear wool socks and
take all three liners with us to the boot store when we are making a
purchase.

Footgear   51

Anyone who wants to make their own liners can get kits from Frostline in Broomfield, Colorado, from Holubar Mountaineering or Altra at Boulder, Colorado, from Sundown at Burnsville, Minnesota, and from Country Ways, Minnetonka, Minnesota. *Wilderness Camping* magazine and *Back Packer* magazine are good sources of information on kits and supplies as well as finished products.

There are down boot liners on the market, and these are allright around camp or cabin, but on the trail they soak up perspiration and soon become useless because they cannot be readily dried.

I am harping a lot on footwear because it is one of our chief problems on the trail and also in search-and-rescue work. Care of boots cannot be overstressed. No matter how tired the party may be at the end of the day, the boots must be dried out so that they will be supple and wearable in the morning. Furthermore, it is good practice to unlace the boots nearly all the way down and spread out the sides and tongue at night so that your foot will slide in even if some moisture is present and the boots are stiff. Once your feet are inside and moving around, the heat they generate will help thaw the boot out.

SPECIAL HEADGEAR

Heads lose as much heat as any other part of the body and they also have three appendages very vulnerable to frostbite: the nose and the two ears. Ordinary knit caps that pull down over the ears are good protection inside a wind parka hood. The Balaclava-style headgear favored by many campers also offers good protection. Headbands may suffice on still, warm days on a ski slope, but they are not much good in very cold, windy, trail situations. Face masks are not as stylish as goggles and knit caps, but goggles will not keep frostbite off the nose, cheeks and chin.

When it is way below zero we sometimes use a long knit scarf which can be wrapped around to form a face mask or used as a supplement to the mask. The scarf can also be brought around the neck to cover the upper chest. Layering off, the scarf is removed first, then the face mask, then the parka hood is flipped back, then the cap is rolled up a little at a time to release heat through the ears. We never ski or snowshoe with the cap off entirely because this releases heat too fast and burns up far too much energy. We keep the cap on and layer off the body garments.

5: Clothing for Winter Camping

THE "CHIMNEY" EFFECT

In addition to adding or subtracting clothing layers in order to adjust insulation, individual clothing items can be tightened or loosened to create temperature changes within the layers. Since all heat, including body heat, rises, loosening clothing at the neck will allow heat and moisture to escape. This will occur slowly if the waist cord and cuffs are tight. If the neck, cuffs and waist of a wind parka are all loosened, cool air will enter below the hips and at the wrists and will circulate upward and out the neck, taking heat and moisture with it. This is known as the "chimney" effect. Some circulation occurs both ways through the sleeves, but the main draft is out at the neck. In addition, the shirt neck can be opened wide, letting more body heat escape, if desired.

The trick is to start loosening garments when the body heat begins to build, but well before perspiration becomes a problem. By carefully adjusting the apertures, you can control the amount of draft, just as you do on a small wood stove, and a comfortable temperature can be maintained.

OUTFITS FOR CAMP

When he reaches a campsite, two things are usually occurring simultaneously to chill the traveller: He is exerting less, allowing his body to cool rapidly, and night is approaching and the outside temperature is plummeting.

While we are still warm from the trail, we try to get the wood gathered, a warming fire started and the tent up. But the minute we begin to feel the chill, we break open the packs and slip into warm, dry clothes. A pole platform or a bit of canvas placed on top of the snow in front of the warming fire makes a nice place to stand while changing clothes. We do this usually starting at the top.

Headgear

Although the knit cap is good for trail travel, we have found that an insulated or wool earflapper cap holds the heat and protects the ears when we are less active. It weighs only a few ounces and is a comfortable replacement for a damp knit cap or headband.

Body Cover

Now that big, fluffy down or synthetic fiber parka comes into use. We pull off the wind parka and whatever else we are wearing down to the shirt, then zip into that dry, comfortable, quilted cover that insulates the body completely no matter what the temperature does. If the underwear and shirt are damp from perspiration, that big parka will still retain the heat and even absorb some of the moisture, as long as the camper does not engage in some frantic activity and start sweating all over again.

Hands

Mittens tend to get wet during the day and an extra pair of mittens or just an extra set of dry knit liners is handy. As the temperature drops in the late afternoon, wet leather gloves or mittens will begin to stiffen and ice up, making it awkward to do chores. Sometimes we wear only the knit gloves and knit mittens while erecting camp, at least until we can get the leather mittens dried out and supple again.

Legs and Feet

Any problems with pants, socks and boots are all handled at the same time since the boots have to be pulled off anyway to take off iced-up pants or damp underwear. As soon as the boots are off (while standing on the tarp or pole platform by the fire), dry socks replace the damp ones from the day, along with dry boot liners if necessary. The wind pants, if not already layered off, can be removed to allow some circulation and drying through the wool pants. Unless the camp is in an exposed, windy area where it shouldn't be, wool pants over long johns should be warm enough, particularly with the thick parka hanging down well past the mid-section. For the past two years we have been experimenting with Polarguard bib overalls, built with a ripstop nylon inner and outer shell, for camp use. We sew two-way zippers on the inner seam of each pant leg to provide ventilation and also to allow room to pull the overalls on or off without taking off our boots. The seat and knees are reinforced with Cordura to resist wear. We can also turn these padded pants around at night, putting the bib in the back to protect the kidneys from the cold, and use them as a sleeping bag liner. This means that in many weather conditions we can use a single Polarguard sleeping bag instead of a double bag. Or we can use the pants as a buffer in a double bag in case the temperature goes to 40 or 50 degrees below zero. To our knowledge, these overalls are still in the experimental stage, but one style is available from Sierra Kits, Riverside, California.

If our underwear is wet, we either replace it with the quilted Dacron type or put the Dacron over it so that it will dry out slowly under the wool pants. Anything damp that is not being worn is put to dry by the fire. Some financially stable campers acquire a set of down pants for camp use, and these are certainly functional. If a fire has not been built, you will want to show some alacrity in changing from damp to dry clothes and in getting your boots back on before your knees turn white and your toes curl under.

Ski boots are worthless around camp, and we get out of them quickly and into pacs, mukluks or Indian hightops. If we were wearing pacs during the day, we usually just change socks and liners. In the last few years we have been sewing our own camp mukluks out of heavy nylon, inserting eyelets for laces. We sew on either a double nylon or a buckskin sole, cut a foam insole pad to fit and wear our homemade Polarguard inner liners and wool socks.

Colors

While color is mostly a matter of personal preference, there are some practical reasons for using bright or dark colors. White or yellow parkas and pants may have some advantages when stalking wildlife but they are not easily visible against a background of snow. It is easier to keep tabs on your clothes around camp if they are bright red, blaze orange, blue, dark green, brown or black, and in an emergency it is essential that outer clothing be highly visible from both the ground and the air.

EXTRA CLOTHING

The only extra items necessary are underwear and socks. One additional set of dry underwear may be handy on a trip of over five days and several extra sets of wool socks are required. Socks are continually being soaked and replaced with dry ones. Over a week or so, wool socks may begin to wear through at the heels (or they may get burned up while drying out) and it is good to have at least two extra pair in your pack. There is no reason to haul extra pants, shirts, sweaters or jackets. If these items get wet, they are just dried out. If they get lost, the owner will probably be lost with them and he will have more pressing concerns than changing his wardrobe.

CARE OF CLOTHING

Since the good Lord did not see fit to equip the human animal with fur, it behooves the winter traveller to take good care of his clothing. It is all that stands between him and becoming a partial or entire block of ice. Before any trip, clothing should be inspected and any holes, ripped seams or zipper problems repaired. While worn, tattered and battered outfits may give the impression of trail experience, they also allow body warmth to escape. Clothing should be clean when you start out, since collected dirt and dried-on body oils reduce insulating quality and block moisture release.

On the trail, every attempt is made to keep the outfit as dry as possible. If a spill is taken, outer layers are removed and the snow shaken out before it can turn into water. Gaiters are kept snug, snow kept out of boots. When "brush breaking" through heavy undergrowth where trails are indistinct or missing, it pays to move branches aside rather than bull through them with your torso, and it also pays to keep a sharp eye out for projecting branches or stubs that can snag and rip into a parka or pants. When you are pulling the sled, there should be some slack in your clothing above the harness so that your arms can swing freely and there will be no stress that can tear out parka seams under your armpits. Any rips that do occur should be sewed up promptly when camp is made.

DRYING OUT BY THE FIRE

Wet boots, pants, socks and other items must be handled with care when they are being dried out. We can scarcely recall a trip during which somebody didn't burn the toes out of his socks, a piece of sole from a rubber-bottom pac, the top off a knit cap or even a sleeve from a parka while trying to rush the drying or not being attentive to the fire. It is good practice to build a simple pole drying rack close enough to the fire to catch the heat but not within scorching distance. The rack is lashed up with cord or rope so that it can be untied and dismantled when camp is broken.

The trick in drying is to produce an even intensity of heat. This means that one member of the party is usually in charge. Fires which are allowed to dwindle down to coals then flare up with a new heap of fuel can be particularly damaging to synthetic fiber garments. Socks or mittens can be arranged on sticks stuck into the snow around the fire, but care must be taken that the snow around the sticks doesn't melt, allowing them to topple over. Garments steaming on the drying rack should be constantly turned so that they dry evenly and checked frequently to see that they do not get too hot. Fabrics do not have to come in direct contact with flames to be destroyed. Reflected heat can start wool smoldering or cause synthetics to shrivel.

Boots dry best propped up with the opening toward the fire, laces carefully tucked back so that they don't get scorched. It is poor practice to place boots with their soles to the fire because the heat may melt or burn the soles, and the interior cannot dry until the heat travels clear through the bottoms. Parkas and pants should be continually turned inside and out so that they dry evenly. If there is a breeze, the drying rack is placed on the up-wind side of the fire so that sparks cannot blow into the garments.

Since wood hunting often requires considerable stamping around in deep snow, we turn to and get the entire wood supply hauled in at one time and, insofar as possible, over the same trail. Thus everybody's clothes can be pretty well dried out before bed-time and nobody has to venture forth and get a last accumulation of snow on his pants and boots. Any items left not dried out overnight will probably be quite stiff and unusable in the morning.

Maymayguishi.

All clothing, regardless of how dry it is, is stored under cover for the night. Nothing is left outside where snow can pile up and bury it out of sight. Not only does snow "eat" items left out but anyone who travels the north knows that the *Maymayguishi,* the wee woodland folk of Indian lore, delight in moving items around and hiding them from unwary campers. To thwart the machinations of these invisible, perverse little people, each item of clothing and equipment should have a definite storage place, and when it is not in use should be put back in its niche. *Maymayguishi* do not hide items which are properly stored. They only run off with equipment and clothing which was set aside "just for now."*

In case there are some skeptical readers who demand proof that these super-natural beings exist, we ask them only to wait until they are out in the woods and some item has vanished, then pause for a few moments in silence. High overhead, where the wind is soughing through the spruce tops, he will faintly but clearly hear the Maymayguishi laughing.

6: Equipment for Winter Campers

Essential as it is to travel light in the winter, there are some personal items which each member of the party should have both for comfort and safety. While there will be some duplication and one item might suffice for the whole party, it is good practice for each person to be as self-sufficient as possible even while engaging in a group operation. Some of these items are for the pocket or pouch, some go into the backpack.

POCKET ITEMS

These are articles which come into regular use and which are small enough to be carried on the person without adding undue bulk or weight.

Navigational Aids

Each person should have his own compass and map. The two types of compasses we use most commonly are the Silva and the military lensatic style or something like it. Both of these are almost breakproof, a necessity in tough terrain where spills cannot be avoided and there is a good chance that the instrument will be banged against a tree, a stump or hard ice while riding in a pocket. Cheap, flimsy compasses can be easily broken. Travelling without a compass in strange country is not impossible, but it can be darn uncomfortable.

We carry our compasses in our front pants pockets and have them tethered to our belts with a nylon leash about a foot long, to insure against losing them in a snowdrift during a downhill wipeout. Some campers prefer to carry their compass in a shirt or jacket pocket with a button-up flap with the safety string tied to a buttonhole or snap.

While more than one map may be used on a lengthy trip, the map for the current portion of the trip is carried in a waterproof plastic case in a parka or shirt pocket. The plastic protects the map against wetting by perspiration or melting snow which can blur the ink and melt the paper. I carry mine in my shirt pocket where it is handy to pull out for reference at any time. In addition to the map, we carry a pencil with which we check off landmarks on our map as we pass them and also chart direction lines for shooting compass readings.

Matches

The importance of being able to start a fire quickly in winter is not debatable. Every member of the party carries a waterproof pocket match container or pouch in addition to the group's match supply. We have found that a small, plastic bag makes a good auxiliary match pouch. The matches are bunched inside, the open end folded over, wrapped around the matches and held in place with a big rubber band. Metal match cases, if used, should be kept in an inside pocket. Otherwise a person can get "burnt" fingers trying to open the cold case in below-zero temperatures. We use wooden kitchen matches. Some campers prefer paper book matches because they have a sandpaper striker on the back, but paper matches are easily destroyed by moisture. Finding a striker for wooden matches can present a problem, however, particularly if built-in strikers such as a parka or pants zippers are wet from snow. Match containers with built-in strikers are handy, as is a strip of sandpaper rolled up inside the match container. Dry matches can be struck by popping two heads together. Matches can be waterproofed by dipping them lightly in melted paraffin.

Fire Starter

In the winter it is not enough just to get a match lit. Some sort of tinder is needed to get smaller branches started. We carry a foil pouch of GI fire tablets (Hexamine). A match touched to a tablet will get a flame going on which other tinder and kindling can be stacked. These tablets are fairly windproof and will also take scattered snowflakes without going out. Some campers make their own fire starters by dipping strips of wax paper in melted paraffin and then rolling the strips up to dry in inch-high cylinders. In the outdoor cooking sections at supermarkets, boxes of fire-starting tabs are available along with charcoal and other barbecue supplies. The problem is that these items are only on the shelves when the stores are promoting supplies for summer cookouts. The winter camper should purchase them at that time, since when he needs them in the winter, they are likely to be unavailable. Occasionally they are on sale at GI surplus stores and campers' specialty shops.

Knives

It is fashionable in some circles to travel the north country with a huge belt knife (some look like miniature broad-swords), but these have little utility other than dressing out a moose or bear during hunting season. Either a small belt knife or a pocket knife is much better for handling most camp cutting chores. The one advantage of a sheath knife is that it is at your fingertips and it doesn't have to be unfolded when your fingers are cold. Some of our group prefer folding knives that slip inside their pants pockets. The Swiss Army models, which have a screwdriver, punch and can opener along with the cutting blades, are handy. To make them lighter and flatter, some of my friends pry off the red plastic coating on each side of the metal case. These knives also come equipped with a lanyard shackle which allows them to be lashed to the belt so they won't get dropped in the snow. Before buying a pocket knife, we test the spring to make sure that the blade comes out fairly easily. With cold, numb fingers it is tough enough to get a pocket knife open on the trail without fighting one of those stiff models that almost requires a pair of pliers.

Sunglasses

The importance of protecting your eyes against the glare of the sun on the winter snow cannot be overstressed. Either tinted goggles or glasses will serve this purpose well. We avoid metal frame glasses, at least those having metal which will touch bare flesh alongside the nose, temples and ears. Some campers who have metal frame prescription glasses wrap a few bits of adhesive tape to the frames at points of contact. Goggles have the advantage of shielding the eyes from the sun at the side and they also keep out flying particles of snow. Goggles should have ventilation to prevent fogging up, and it is handy to have along a glycerin stick or some

Tinted glasses (bottom) and snow goggles.

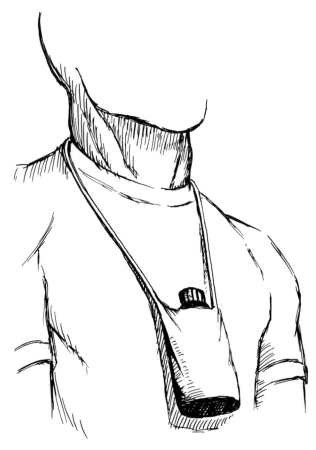

Water bottle slung from neck and held next to body to prevent freezing.

type of anti-fogging cream to rub on the inside of the eye pieces. Goggles and glasses should be tested out in the cold at home before making any trip. They are checked for fit, points of contact with the face and any possible problems with fogging.

Water Bottle

Each member of the party carries his own water bottle on a cord hanging from his neck. This may sound a little bizarre to people who have not spent much time roaming the back country in winter, but a continually available supply of drinking water is a necessity. We use half-pint plastic bottles with screw-on lids that are carried inside the shirt to prevent freezing. As we pause regularly for a sip, more water, ice or snow is added to refill the bottle. Being next to the body, the water is kept fairly warm. When it is consumed, the partially warmed water does not use up as much energy or heat loss from the body as would cold water taken in directly.

Notebook

A journal, however brief, is kept for the trip. In it we jot down landmarks passed, compass courses, lunch stops, campsite locations, weather conditions and any other bits of information as the trip progresses. The journal is used in conjunction with the map and not only furnishes a log for later reference, but also provides pertinent data if some unforseen accident occurs and somebody must go for help.

On most trips we use a small, spiral-bound notebook which fits in a shirt pocket for a journal. Along with trip progress, we evaluate equipment and methods, putting down any suggestions for improvement while they are still fresh in mind.

Long after the trip, when we have evening coffee sessions around the cabin stove, we haul out the journals along with photographic slides and relive the trip, usually with considerable hilarity. On one 1977 trip up the Kekekabic Trail between Ely and Gunflint in Minnesota's Superior National Forest, we were confronted with several downhill situations with nearly impossible turns at the bottom. Trail breaker Andy Hill positioned himself at one critical point with his 35-millimeter Pentax and recorded three spectacular wipeouts as our nine-member group came past, one at a time. We have nearly worn out that sequence, reviewing and checking out ways to improve our technique.

Pocket Kerchief

In cold weather, noses run in the forest just as they do in the city, and one must have something upon which to wipe them. Sleeves and mittens are cold, uncomfortable and certainly untidy. Pocket packets of Kleenex are handy. The individual sheets are stuffed in a pocket after use and burned in the fire at night. For cloth kerchiefs, we prefer the large, bandana-type because they can also be used as outside bandages over a sprain, as slings and as padding. We carry several of these, one in the pocket and a couple in the pack.

Emergency Ration

This is carried in two types: We use a bag of homemade gorp (raisins, nuts, candies) for nibbling during rest stops, and we carry high-energy bars which are not eaten except in a real emergency when nothing else is available. Energy bars or squares of fruitcake can be used when someone gets mixed up and loses the trail or in the event someone must leave the group and head for outside help without being encumbered with a sled and equipment. They are double wrapped in foil to prevent crumbling inside a parka pocket.

Rope and Cord

We have already noted that in some team operations, a coil of light nylon rope may be a handy aid in getting equipment and personnel up or down a steep slope. It can be carried on the back of the belt or in a parka pocket or lashed to the backpack where it will not get snagged in the brush. In addition to the rope, fifty feet of nylon cord can be packed in a coil inside a pants pocket. There are dozens of uses for the cord, including making quick repairs to equipment, for laces, for lashing down loose items and for an extra guy line or two on the tent. Having the cord handy in your pocket saves time hunting through the duffle.

Ointments

Cold is usually accompanied by dryness, and many winter campers have trouble with drying and cracking lips and skin. A pocket tube of Blistex, Chap Stick or some other type of lip salve will prevent the lips from cracking. Such creams as Sea & Ski or Mt. Everest Skreen, applied to the face, will help prevent drying and burning. During most of the winter in the Northland, sunburn is not much of a problem because the major portions of the trips are made through shaded forests. But in late winter and early spring, when there is a hard crust, reflection off the snow is pronounced. Campers who travel the mountains, high above the timberline, are continually exposed to sun and reflected light and apply sunburn cream as a matter of course. The one cream which is not necessary in winter is insect repellent.

Watch

It might appear that the need to tell time, other than by the sun, is unnecessary on a winter trip. In a good many instances some of our party have left their watches home with this thought in mind. However, days are short in winter and it is a good idea to know what time the party got under way, how much time has passed between landmarks in order to judge the group's speed, when snack and water halts should be called, when it is lunchtime, when it is time to start looking for an evening campsite and when it is time to go to bed. Either a wristwatch or a pocket watch on a lanyard will work, but they must be kept wound. If a watch stops out in the bush there is no television, radio or electric clock on the wall to set it by.

BACKPACK OR SLED ITEMS

There are some personal items which are not needed regularly during the day but are nevertheless essential. These are carried in the backpack or on the cross-country sled.

Toilet Kit

Of the three essentials for winter camping success—warmth, dryness, and cleanliness—the third item is one of the most overlooked.

Some winter campers labor under the delusion that anyone who goes on such a trip should return with a face full of dirty whiskers and a generally scruffy look, as though he had just conquered the Himalayas. In explanation, it is held either that nobody really gets dirty in the snow or that keeping clean is simply too difficult in cold weather. Neither is true. Travelling a trail on snow and ice requires more exertion than hiking the same distance in warm weather on a dry trail. Furthermore, in cold weather the body is more heavily encased in clothing. Perspiration releases body oils and builds up as the body sweats and dries, over and over. In a few days, the unwashed camper begins to emit an aroma like that of a defunct goat. If it doesn't bother the individual, it will certainly bother his tent mates, since human olfactory senses tune in more acutely on someone else. Therefore we wash. It is even possible to take a sponge bath with hot water, bathing a little of the torso at a time. As one bushwhacker puts it: "I wash as far down as possible, then as far up as possible . . . and then I wash Old Possible."

Brushing the teeth is no great chore and it refreshes the mouth as well as being hygienic. Some of us shave on the trail. This may be heresy to many of our younger, bushier trail pounders to whom a full set of chin whiskers is a macho must. However, we have seen many times when our bearded comrades spent considerable time at the end of the day trying to separate their face masks from their frozen beards. Beards collect ice. In a face-freezing situation, when a warm bare hand on a chin or jaw can nip frostbite in the bud, a beard full of ice can prevent immediate treatment. To the guy who likes a beard in the winter and is willing to put up with all the inconvenience and discomfort, I say, have at it. Me? I shave out of a tin of hot water. My toilet kit contains a razor and blades, a bar of face soap (which also lathers up for shaving soap), toothbrush and toothpowder (paste will freeze), a washcloth, towel and a mirror. The mirror doubles as a candle reflector for reading inside the tent at night and can also be used for signalling during rescue work.

Sewing Kit

Repairs to clothing are more essential during a winter camping trip than in the summer. On a warm weather backpacking jaunt, torn pants or jackets merely flap in the breeze. In the winter, they let the cold in and the heat out. We pack three or four different sizes of needles, a thimble, a spool of No. 60 thread and a heavy-duty polyester thread. The thread is removed from the spool before the trip and rolled onto a flat piece of cardboard, making it much easier and more compact to pack. Added to the kit are some buttons along with a few large- and medium-size safety pins. The whole works is laid inside a square of nylon patching material, rolled up into a small package and secured with a cord or rubber band.

Camera

It is seldom on any winter trip that we do not have at least two cameras along. One is always used for shooting transparencies and we sometimes use one for taking black-and-white photos. The greatest concern with any camera is packing it so that it will not be damaged. There are some excellent metal-covered cases on the market which will protect the unit from anything short of a direct hit by an anti-tank shell, and we have hauled these on the sleds. The problem with these is that when a spectacular photo situation arises on the trail, the sled has to be unpacked to get at the camera. In flat country or while travelling across frozen lakes and rivers, we sometimes carry the camera inside the wind parka, the strap around our necks. But in rough country the risk of falling face down on the camera is too great. We have found another way, and that is to roll the camera up inside the parka which is stuffed in the backpack. Since we have little else in the pack except bedding and clothing, it is easy to locate the camera, pull it out for the picture and return it to padded safety.

Binoculars

I never carry these but some of the people I go into the woods with would never consider leaving theirs at home. The popular binoculars in the 7-by-35 range are fairly bulky and run well over a pound in weight. For the inveterate bird watcher or nature student, one of the new 7- or 8-power monoculars by Bushnell or Pentax can be more easily packed, or even carried in a pocket. They weigh just four ounces and are about four inches long.

Survival Kits

Within the past few years a whole buzzard's nest of items have been listed in advertisements under the heading of "survival." Generally these kits are built around some sort of a plastic shelter like a tube tent and include matches, a candle, wire, beverage,

whistle, mirror, instruction booklet and a can to pack it all in
. . . the can doubling as a water pot. To this may be added an
aluminized plastic blanket. There is nothing wrong with these kits
and they have been used by hunters or hikers lost in the woods.
However, we have the same or better items already in our outfit
and the only time we are separated by even a short distance from
them is when we are in camp at night. The whistle we usually
carry on search-and-rescue missions for signalling and some campers carry them all the time. I don't, but maybe I should.

Books

It may sound a little silly to suggest hauling along some reading
material, but reading is one of the best recreational pursuits in the
winter camp. Night comes very early and once supper is over
there is little activity outside the tent except fireside sessions and
drying out clothes. Once all of the stories have been twice retold,
there is little else to do but crawl into bed. It might seem like a
dandy time to catch up on some back sleep and this can be the
case; however, the guy who goes to bed at eight o'clock figuring on
getting ten hours or so sleep will discover his kidneys are calling
him to account about 4 A.M., which is a very dark and unlovely
time to step outside in the cold. So we read for a few hours before
going to sleep, making a final latrine trip just before blowing out
the candle. Since I am not a speed reader, it takes me about three
nights to get through an ordinary paperback. Two books will
handle most trips since I can trade with somebody else when my
material runs out.

Billfold

There is not much a person can buy with either cash or a credit
card out in the wilderness, but there are items which need to be
carried somewhere, including identification and any licenses or
camping permits required by state or provincial governments. Because of perspiration, billfolds can take a beating on a winter trip
and cards can get soaked. Sometimes we use a cheap, dime store
wallet for our necessary papers and leave our regular billfold with
all its contents at home or with someone at the point of access for
the trip. It does not pay to leave billfolds locked in the glove com-

partments of autos left on remote roads. At one time they would have been safe, but not any more.

Flashlight

A plastic flashlight is usually preferred over metal because there is less chance of getting frostbitten fingers from grabbing it accidentally. We keep the batteries in our pants pockets in camp to keep them warm. If the batteries get cold, the light will be dim.

Ice chisel with sheath.

7: Planning the Trip

※※

To the person not oriented to snow travel, it is nearly impossible to describe one's sense of buoyant anticipation as the loads are finally lashed tight, mittens grip the ski poles and the trip gets under way in the crisp dawn. The only sound is the rhythmic *shush* of snowshoes or the hissing of crystals under skis as dawn pokes a reddish eye over the rim of a frozen world, casts a rosy reflection on the dark tips of pine and spruce and sends long fingers of blue shadow reaching across the unbroken snow. Civilization vanishes as though it never existed. Mobile and self-contained, we push off with confidence, eager to meet any challenge on the adventure ahead. Our confidence is based on the knowledge that we are adequately prepared for the trip. Preparation and close attention to detail are the keys to any winter campout.

WHO GOES?

It is a good idea for trip leaders or organizers to be quite careful whom they include in the venture. There are some very mellow folk who will jump at the chance to try anything new and may even "talk" a good trip until the moment of truth arrives and it is discovered that they lack knowhow, proper equipment or both. On the other hand, some skilled skiers, snowshoers and campers are anything but mellow, and the leader should also be wary of them. Quite often it isn't the big things such as tough weather that shreds the fabric of a winter venture. It can be a little thing like one guy who snores. We have seen more than one camping trip come unstitched because a nasal virtuoso made the tent walls billow with his renditions. Silly? Not a bit. Good camping companions are not easy to come by and in winter, when even more togetherness is required, it pays to be choosey.

We tend to look for specialists on our outings, such as a person who is up on first aid, one who is an ace at repairing gear, one who is a good cook and food organizer, one who is a sharp navigator by map and compass. A good winter trip is built around a nucleus of experienced people. Beyond that you pays your money and you takes your chances.

INITIAL EQUIPMENT CHECK

Everyone involved in the trip should be brought together under one roof for at least one and possibly more sessions to make certain that the entire group is properly equipped. We like to gather around the kitchen table at night, a big pot of coffee steaming on the stove, maps spread flat, everybody working on routes and lists with pen or pencil. First it must be determined how many tents will be needed, who has them and who will be sleeping in each tent. Once this is worked out, sled teams can be planned around each tent unit.

We usually put one person in charge of getting the maps, one in charge of the food and one in charge of checking out the gear. It is the job of the gear leader to make sure that the sleds, tents, tarps and other group items are assembled, and to check out each person's individual equipment and clothing. One way to do this is go down a list at the group get-together, taking one item at a time, something like this:

"O.K., how do we stack up on bags and mats, Joe?"

"Goose down and Ensolite."

"Don?"

"Polarguard and two-inch foam."

"Scrap the foam. Anybody else got an extra Ensolite pad?"

"Yeh, I have."

"O.K., Don, get that pad from Eddie."

And so on through each item of gear and wearing apparel. It may be suggested that each member of the party copy down the list so that he can do his own checking when he gets home. Special attention should be given to foot gear, making sure that each person has adequate boots for the trail as well as for camp. There is not much margin for mistake here and letting something slip by is good neither for the individual nor for the group. If, for instance, somebody's boots are not in good condition, that person should be given the choice of getting the right outfit or passing up the trip. If he runs into frostbite, he isn't the only one who will have to suffer. It will be up to the group to abort their trip and haul him out of the woods.

If the trip includes ice fishing, as many of ours do, the best fishermen lay out the tackle needed (which is usually very simple in the winter) and make provision for somebody to acquire any necessary bait. The question of who is bringing cameras should be discussed to make sure the trip is recorded on film and to eliminate a lot of duplicate picture taking.

Food List

Although the subject of food will be taken up in Chapter IX, it should be noted here that advance planning calls for measuring provisions in proportion to the number of people and days out. Just about anybody in our group can handle this since we are nearly all canoe guides in the summer and have a pretty good idea of how much individuals consume on the trail. But even for the uninitiated, it is not difficult to order food. Almost everything on the grocer's shelves today is made up conveniently into serving units of various sizes. Oatmeal can be purchased in individual packets and, as a rule of thumb, two or three packets will make one breakfast, depending on who is eating and what else is being served. Soups, bouillon, coffee, tea, Tang and chocolate also come in individual packets.

If there is a camping or backpacker's specialty shop in town, it is a good bet that it carries a supply of dehydrated and freeze-dried trail food, made up in two-, four- or six-man units. These require only the addition of hot water to be made ready to eat. What the person in charge of ordering food must do is find out if anyone in the party has any violent dislikes or allergies to any particular foods. Obviously, it is not always possible to get universal agreement, but a majority agreement will usually do. Once a reasonable menu is assembled, it is the job of the food chief to make the purchase and divide the costs.

In some cases, various members of the group may contribute items, particularly if meals are precooked at home and frozen for the trip. I usually bake up a bunch of bannock as part of my contribution to the sortie. When meals are being cooked and frozen ahead of time, either the chore can be parcelled out or a couple of volunteers can make all the meals up. These costs, too, should be computed and prorated among the group.

In estimating menus, it pays to go somewhat overboard on beverages. Thirst is a constant companion in the winter and a whole lot of drinks are consumed during a day on the trail and at night in camp. Let's look at a typical day's liquid intake. For breakfast each individual will have at least two cups of a hot beverage, maybe four. Figure two for the lunch stop on the trail, one while supper is getting ready, two with supper and one after supper. That comes to eight cups or two quarts of hot drink for one day. Since this is the minimum liquid intake each person should have for one day, that is a conservative figure. Let's say there are six people in the party and each person has the following: two hot Tang, two tea for breakfast; two hot chocolate for lunch; four coffee for supper. For the six this tallies up to twelve individual Tang packets, twelve individual instant tea packets, twelve hot chocolate and twenty-four instant coffee or Sanka packets. Now take this figure for a week and it totals eighty-four Tang, eighty-four tea, eighty-four chocolate and 168 coffee. And if half the party likes cream and sugar in their coffee, we have another eighty-four packets of each of these items to include. It will not be any great problem if there are a few beverage packets left over, but heaven help the food chief if he has some veteran coffee drinkers along and the group runs out of coffee two nights before the end of the trip!

In any event, we usually throw in enough instant soups and beverages to carry the group for at least two extra meals beyond the estimated length of the trip in case of a weather hangup or some unforseen impediment that slows up progress.

Test Run

With the bulk of the planning arranged, it is always a good idea for the group to take a one-day tour, particularly if there is a newcomer or two who hasn't been out with the group before. This gives the entire party an opportunity to determine each individual's speed, endurance and attitude before getting committed to an overnight campout. If a ski trip is planned, each member can take a turn breaking trail and setting the pace. The technique of each member can be readily observed. If somebody is having difficulty, the group can be certain that the difficulty will blossom into real trouble with the addition of a loaded backpack or trail sled. Usually an individual will cut himself out of the party if he discovers that he is running hopelessly behind. If he doesn't, the group can gently inform him that "maybe you should spend some more time on your technique and go with us on the next campout." It pays to be firm on this point or else become resigned to a slower trip with the rest of the group shouldering most of the load.

The test run idea is also important when you are snowshoeing. A good segment of the outdoor public thinks that snowshoes are just something you put on to walk over the top of the snow. It is amazing the number of adventurous souls who will volunteer to go on a snowshoe trip without any prior experience on the webs. A trial run will usually settle this issue. Even if the inexperienced snowshoer has enough technique to get by, it will be only a matter of a few hours before he will begin to complain about pains on the inside of his thighs. By night, he may be a basket case.

On the other hand, if the majority of the group are novice skiers or snowshoers, it merely means that the trip should be shortened considerably, maybe to three to five miles each day on skis or one to two miles on snowshoes, with at least a one-day rest in the middle. Somebody is sure to comment, "Boy, what a trip . . . a couple of miles a day." So? If the object is to have fun and camp out in the snow, it doesn't make any difference if the group is two miles from the nearest road or two hundred. The trip doesn't have to be an expedition to be enjoyable.

PLOTTING THE ROUTE

We use large-scale topographic maps, the best we can locate. The U.S. Geological Survey maps are excellent and are often sold by ski shops and outfitters in remote country. They are also available directly from the U.S. Geological Survey at two addresses: at 1200 S. Eads St., Arlington, Virginia 22202, for areas east of the Mississippi River, and at the Federal Center, Denver, Colorado 80225, for areas west of the Mississippi. For Canada, the best source is the Canada Map Office, 615 Booth St., Ottawa, Ontario K1A 0E9. A letter to any of these agencies will bring a list of the maps available for any area and also information on the scales in which maps can be obtained. All of Canada has been mapped in the 1:250,000 scale (1 inch equals 4 miles), which is pretty short on detail for ordinary recreational travel unless the camper is already acquainted with the area. Better are the 1:50,000 scale maps (1¼ inch equals 1 mile), which are printed for many Canadian areas. The U.S. Geological Survey has maps in 1:62,500 scale (1 inch to 1 mile), which is a handy pocket size. We have also used some big 1:24,000 scale maps (2½ inches to 1 mile), which are very easy to read but somewhat bulky. We prefer to have one set of large-scale maps for the entire party and have each member carry his own 1:62,500 map. Many state and federal parks, recreation and wilderness areas have good trail maps available. These can be obtained in advance by writing to state conservation departments or to the headquarters of the area you are interested in.

The importance of the topographic type of map for winter camping must be stressed. These maps show the surface relief of an area with contour lines, and also show important features such as lakes, streams, marshes, roads and settlements, which furnish the traveller with valuable landmarks necessary for winter navigation. There are some maps used by summer hikers which show trails and points of interest, but do not show the contour of the terrain. These can be misleading in the winter, since snow obliterates most indications of foot trails and the skier or snowshoer has only the natural features of the countryside for his guide.

In much of the country we travel in the North, there are broad expanses of frozen lakes with interconnecting portage trails that serve as snowy corridors. We look for such features on our area maps. We also follow frozen river courses, cross muskeg meadows which are impassable in the summer, and trek ridges where timber is thin enough to allow passage. On our maps we judge the terrain by our own ability and set up in advance reasonable distances for daily travel. Under most local conditions, with full loads, we figure five to seven miles per day on snowshoes and from eight to fifteen on skis. On the map we plot not only each day's course, but also each night's campsite which we plan to reach in late afternoon while there is still ample daylight to make camp. If we are going into unfamiliar country, we rule in lines between landmarks and jot down the lines' compass bearings for quick reference when we get there. On a sub-zero day it is often a cumbersome task to make a pencil function with numb fingers.

Local Sources

Over much of the north country, in both the U.S. and Canada, there are Chambers of Commerce and Tourist Associations which carry information on local trails, tours and accommodations. While most resorts are summer operations, a few are geared up for winter activities, and some even specialize in snow sports. Outdoor and travel magazines carry the addresses of area tourist associations. The information is also available through the travel departments of state and provincial governments. The sportsmen's shows and ski shows that appear in the major cities each year are places where one can make personal contact to acquire information on specific areas.

Prior to heading into an unfamiliar area, it is wise to have accommodations reserved at a motel or resort which can be used as a base of operation. On most trips, the group will need a place to stay overnight to pack as well as some point of return. Most tourist towns are bright spots of life on the cold winter landscape, and a hot shower, a dinner and a night on the town after a trip are excellent ways to alleviate any aches, pains or mental frostbite. More important, having a local address to check in and out of gives the camping party a location to park cars, store excess luggage and leave a travel plan in the event of emergency. When making a reservation with a tourist facility, you can include a letter asking who in that area would have information on trail conditions and campsites.

As much advance information as possible about your intended camping area should be gathered and incorporated in the initial mapping and planning. If the group can arrange to arrive in the area on the afternoon before the trip, a visit to the nearest ski shop may provide contact with ski clubs whose members are familiar with the good routes. The shops themselves sometimes have excellent trail information and maps. Resorts that cater to winter sports may have good trail information and some have guides or tour leaders who have an intimate knowledge of the country. State and

7: *Planning the Trip*

federal rangers in parks and forests are also valuable sources and many of them are avid winter travellers.

There is nothing the dedicated winter sports enthusiast enjoys more than talking shop with kindred souls. A polite inquiry, map in hand, will often bring as much information as can be readily absorbed. This can include some valuable tips such as danger spots along streams, good campsites with adjacent spring holes where ice need not be chopped for a water supply, brushed-out trails with good slopes that may not appear on area maps, ice fishing lakes (although this is not as easy to get out of local folks as trail information), points of scenic or historical interest and areas where wildlife may be observed. In the mountains, avalanche areas can be determined. It is worthwhile to get the best available weather reports for that area in the time of your trip, so that any approaching storm may be noted and planned for, or the trip delayed to avoid it. In areas where it is not advisable to leave a car or van in the woods for a period of time, transportation to and from the access point can be arranged.

It may be appropriate to point out that there are unreliable local sources of information as well as good ones. Sticking to the resorts, ski shops and government personnel is usually a safe bet, but in every area there is at least one local "expert" whose main contribution to outdoor recreation is an excess of hot air. The trouble with these enthusiastic founts of fiction is that they are usually looking for a stranger upon whom to unload their knowledge . . . and a lot of them sound quite convincing. Once, in earlier days, I listened to a kindly, white-haired old gentleman of eighty-plus years relate in infinite detail a dog sled trip he took with two companions into the Klondike during the Gold Rush. His clear, blue eyes sparkled as he told of their hardships on the trail, their efforts to glean the yellow metal from the unforgiving terrain and their final defeat by the elements, followed by a retreat to civilization made possible only by consuming their sled dogs, one by one. It was an absorbing tale of hardship and perseverance. A short time later I met the son of this senior citizen and remarked about the ordeal his father had been through. "You mean old Steve?" he laughed. "Heck, he ain't ever been out of Minnesota."

If there is a moral here, it is not to accept as gospel all information offered on the local level. Sometimes the local source will paint a picture of trail horrors and dire peril which never existed.

And sometimes he may make a trip sound like a piece of cake when it's really a toughie. In such cases it pays to ask your informant: When were you over the trail last? What kind of skis, snowshoes and equipment did you use? What time of the year was it? Who went with you? Is that person still around town? A few penetrating questions will establish whether the informant knows what he is talking about. If he doesn't, he will suddenly become vague on details or beg off that he has "something else to do." In either case, several sources are better than one.

Printed Sources

There are some good tips on winter trips printed in such periodicals as *Wilderness Camping* magazine, 1597 Union St., Schenectady, N.Y. 12309, and *Back Packer* magazine at 28 West 44th St., New York, N.Y. 10036. These publications tell it "like it is" and include some good evaluations of outdoor equipment tested under trail conditions.

Final Details

In some national forests and wilderness areas camping permits are required. Some of these areas have a fee, although usually this is for summer campers and is not required in the winter. Winter camping use is minimal in many areas and the headquarters may not be open on weekends. Provision must be made to handle any necessary paperwork to avoid a last-minute hangup when everyone is itching to shove off. An inquiry sent in advance, asking for details and specifying the date of the proposed trip, will bring the necessary information on what permits are needed and where to obtain them. Obtaining a permit may involve just a simple thing like driving out to a ranger's home on the edge of town, but if you don't know how to do it, a lot of valuable time can be wasted chasing around to get clearance.

It does not pay to go into restricted areas without permits. Very often the permits are free but the fine for not having one is fairly stiff. If fishing is a part of the program, all necessary licenses must be purchased in advance. This is another item to get nailed down when you are sending inquiries to tourist or government agencies. It does not pay to try to slip by without a license on the assumption

The author on the trail with light pack and cross-country sled.

that no game warden will be out in the boonies in midwinter. At least don't try it in Minnesota or Ontario. I know some of the conservation officers in those areas personally, and they turn up in some surprising places. Much of the winter patrolling in the back country is done by 180 Cessnas equipped with skis. While that plane may look like an insignificant silver dot just above the horizon, the officer inside it is carefully scrutinizing the lake surfaces with powerful binoculars. This surveillance has another side. In addition to seeing violations, the wardens are also quick to spot trouble and will be down in an instant if it appears a party needs help.

With all necessary papers and licenses acquired the final packing job is done using an equipment check list. It is a maxim among professional guides and outfitters that no one always remembers every item no matter how many times he packs out. The check list

Information Sources   79

is essential and each item is marked off with a pencil as it is packed.

The last task before departure is to make sure someone—a resort or motel owner, ranger, friend, policeman, gas station operator—has a written itinerary of the trip with names and addresses of campers, route taken and dates of departure and return. If the party is driving its own vehicle to an access point, a note with pertinent information should be folded up and stuck under the windshield wiper. Sheriff's police routinely check parked vehicles and the note will give them a clue if the party is overdue. In most northern areas, the sheriff's police are tied in directly with county search-and-rescue units. Seeing a vacant car parked over a period of days will often cause police to check on the owner and his home address through the license plate and make a phone call to his home. If there is a note stuck on the windshield, such a call will not be made unless the party is overdue. But without a note, the police may call before the scheduled end of the trip and such a phone call to the people at home can be quite upsetting, even though the party camping out is having a fine experience with no problems at all. It just saves all kinds of problems to put a note on the windshield and also to leave word with some contact nearby.

8: On the Trail

There are some people who can wake up in the morning when they want to. A lot of us who served in the Armed Forces have this habit. But it isn't foolproof. Two years ago on a camping trip, I woke up when the moon was creating so much light that I thought it was near dawn and roused the whole camp to start breakfast. It was 3 A.M. There are a few of my friends who are fond of recalling this incident when there is a sufficient audience.

The sun comes up quite late in the winter, and unless your kidneys make the sleeping bag unbearable, it is quite possible to remain asleep or half asleep well into the morning, especially after a strenuous day bucking deep snow. It is a good idea for several members of the party to have watches and if somebody has one of those small travelling alarm clocks, so much the better. Daylight is breaking, or close to it, by 7 A.M. in the winter, so we usually plan to roll out at 6 A.M.—at least the cook should be moving by that time.

BREAKING CAMP

There is probably more time wasted in the morning, rolling up the outfit and getting under way, than is wasted in all the rest of the delays put together. Experienced campers work out some type of system to cut down on the time loss. Everybody has his own method, but ours goes something like this:

Breakfast

There is one designated cook. His job is to: (1) Get the lantern going; (2) Get the stove going; (3) Get a pan of water heating; (4) Lay out the ingredients for breakfast; and (5) Get the rest of the food packed in the sled to move out.

Bags, Interior Gear

Sleeping bags and mats are hung on a rope or frame to air while the rest of the personal gear and clothing is being cleaned out of the tent. If there is wet or frozen clothing, an open fire is kindled and everything dried or at least thawed so that it can be worn or packed.

Tents

Tent flies are carefully unlashed and lifted off the tent to remove as much snow and collected ice crystals as possible. The flies are shaken out and folded. If the tent has a flannel liner, this is removed and shaken out before it is folded up. The tent is unzipped at the door, and the poles are taken down and put in the sled in their bag. Snow anchors or flukes are banged against nearby trees to remove packed snow, and the ropes are cleaned off. By lifting the back of the tent at the corners, you can shake all the bits of snow, ice, leaves or twigs that might be inside down and out the doorway. If the tent has a single tunnel entrance through the vestibule it may be necessary to sweep it down from the inside with the whisk broom and remove the trash by hand before taking out the poles or dropping the guy lines. Once the inside is clean, we fold the floor in half and, with one person on each side, hold it above the snow while a third person sweeps off the loose snow beneath. That completed, the tent and fly are folded up, tied and stowed in the sled.

Kitchen Tarp

On a snowy day, the last item pulled down is the kitchen tarp. The sleeping bags, hung underneath to air, are then punched into their stuff bags. Foam mats are shaken out, rolled up and stuffed into backpacks or lashed on outside the packs. On a clear morning, the tarp may be dropped on a tent site and used as a platform for rolling up bags and other gear. In a well-organized camp, most of the gear will be stowed by breakfast time and there will be little left after breakfast except the stove, lantern and cook pots.

Put Out the Fire

There is an assumption that forest fires cannot start in the winter. It is true that fire will not travel over the snowy surface and there is little likelihood of its getting into the trees, but it can go down into the forest root system. In a very dry season, snow cover notwithstanding, duff and porous root systems can be ignited from a fire above which can burn underground for weeks, popping out in the spring. Fires should be built on rock or mineral soil, if this can be determined when the ground is frozen. Fires should be doused with water and then packed over with snow. If it appears that a fire is burning a hole into the ground, it should be moved to a better site. The hole should then be filled with water and stirred with a stick until all smoke disappears.

Once Around

After camp is tidied up, the biffy covered, the sled and packs loaded and the teams ready to move out, one or two members of the group take a walk "once around" the campsite to make sure nothing is left hanging on a tree or sticking up out of the snow. It is almost certain that such an inspection will reveal a pair of sunglasses, a mitten liner, a frozen sock or some other item . . . right where the Maymayguishi put it.

ON THE MOVE

The group hits the trail with a lightly loaded trail breaker in front followed by a "sled mule" with his sled and perhaps an anchor man behind (if the group is operating three men to a sled). With two-man teams, the trail breaker for the second team acts as anchor man for the first team. Jobs are alternated every hour to spread the work load around.

The lead team should be the most experienced, the most familiar with the area or the best map and compass readers. Even a person who knows a trail intimately in the summer can be misled in the winter. Small streams vanish under the drifts and become merely featureless snow-filled ravines. Foot trails are often indistinguishable from drifted over game trails unless there are blaze marks on the trees to read. Snow-covered marshes or flat meadows may look like ponds or lakes. Patches of deciduous trees that were solid green in the summer are now bunches of black sticks on a white hillside. Winter can be a fooler, and that's why we pay close attention to the map and compass.

Map Reading

Our topographic maps not only give us the flat picture from above—the locations of lakes, streams and trails—but also indicate the surface view from the side, with hills and valleys indicated by brown contour lines. A close look will reveal that some of the lines are heavier than others and are numbered, the figure showing the height above sea level. Where sea level is in regard to where you are standing in the snow is not of any great importance, but noting altitudes above sea level puts all the terrain into the same relationship. A heavy line may read 1500. Wherever that line runs the terrain is 1500 feet above sea level. The next heavy line down will read 1400 (on our 1:62,500-scale map). The space between the numbered lines represents a slope with a 100-foot drop. In between the heavy lines are four fine contour lines, each indicating a 20-foot drop. This interval between lines is printed on the map just under the scale of miles: "Contour interval at 20 feet."

The contour lines show us not only differences in height, but also steepness. A series of lines jammed close together shows a very steep ridge or canyon. Widely meandering contour lines, spread far apart, indicate flatland. What the contour lines do not show, however, is what is on top of the land. Flatland may look nice on a map but it could be covered by an impenetrable patch of spruce. A high ridge may show a hefty climb, but there could be a good trail right up and over the top. This is one reason you should get the best trail information available before setting out.

You should remember that map contours differ. On Canadian 1:50,000 maps the contour interval may be twenty-five or fifty feet, rather than twenty. The peaks and valleys will be shown with fewer lines on these maps. This situation is further complicated where I live on the Minnesota–Ontario border. Canadian maps of this area show a fifty-foot interval on their side and forty-foot on the U.S. side, both on the same map. This is no earth-shaking issue, but the map reader must take careful note of the contour interval, particularly when switching from one map scale to another. It takes practice, which is why one should start winter camping with short trips in familiar country before attempting wilderness jaunts.

Maps should be kept dry. Maps are made of paper and they will deteriorate rapidly when wet. On the trip, they are kept in a plas-

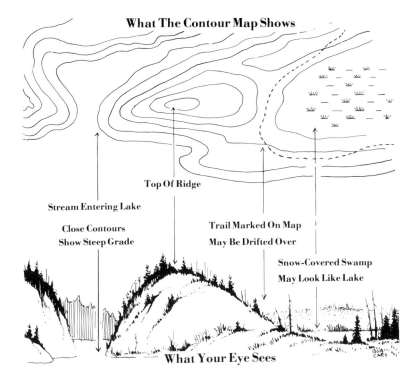

What The Contour Map Shows

Top Of Ridge

Stream Entering Lake

**Close Contours
Show Steep Grade**

**Trail Marked On Map
May Be Drifted Over**

**Snow-Covered Swamp
May Look Like Lake**

What Your Eye Sees

Contour lines on topographic map (above) and the terrain
to which they correspond.

tic envelope away from snow and perspiration.

En route, the map is referred to constantly, at least at every
hour break. Each landmark (stream, pond, lakeshore, island, cliff,
rapids, peak, road, cross trail, cabin) is marked in with a pencil as
it is passed. In the event of a snowstorm that blots out your vision,
or if the map and terrain suddenly do not match up, it is good to
know exactly where your last landmark is located.

If the map and terrain do not match up, stop. Look for some
feature nearby—pond, lake, stream, peak—that can be identified,
and try and locate this on the map. If nothing fits, backtrack. One
of the nice things about winter travel is that no matter where you
go, you leave a trail behind in the snow, a visible link to where you
just came from.

Map Reading   85

Compass

Anyone who goes into the woods without a compass and a working knowledge of how it operates is simply hunting trouble. There are some woodsmen who brag that they never carry a compass. This indicates either: (1) That they spend their time in familiar country where they know the lay of the land; (2) That they are good at reading directions by other means such as the sun; or (3) That they have been darned lucky. Search-and-rescue teams occasionally turn up a lost soul who has a compass but just never learned how to use it.

A compass does not point north. This is the first mental block that must be overcome in regard to compass reading. The needle points to "magnetic north," which is a point currently on Bathurst Island in the Arctic Ocean, about a thousand miles south of the geographic North Pole. The Magnetic pole is a point at which the magnetic lines of the earth meet. Our compass needles follow these magnetic lines. Maps, however, are drawn to true or geographic north. They have meridian lines from top to bottom which are geographic north–south lines. The snow traveller must convert the map course to a compass course.

As noted, magnetic north lies south of true north. Not far from where I live flows the Pigeon River, which marks the border between the U.S. and Canada. This also happens to be a point at which true north and magnetic north are in almost direct line. Thus anyone using a compass around Pigeon River will be reading pretty close to true north right off his compass. However, moving any distance east or west changes this situation dramatically. In the northeastern U.S., a compass needle will point eighteen degrees or more west of true north. In Alaska, it may point forty-five degrees east of north. The difference between true or "map" north and magnetic north is called the "compass declination." Luckily for all of us, it is printed on each map in the margin as a little V-shaped symbol giving the degree of variation. Attempting to follow a compass without correcting for this variation will get a person "loster than lost."

Now let's see how this works out on a trip. Let's say we are at a bend of river A and and we want to get to lake B, five miles away. We lay our Silva Compass on the map, and using the plastic edge for a ruler, draw a line from A to B. At this point we ignore that wiggling compass needle. Next, with the map flat, we rotate the

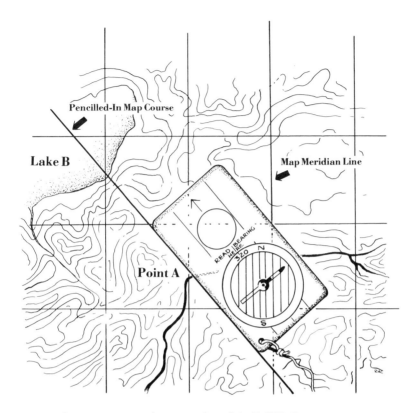

Use of Silva compass to plot course from A to B. With the compass
aligned with the north-south map meridian lines, the bearing of
course AB is 320 degrees.

movable compass dial until the "N" is pointed north on the map
and one of the little lines inside the dial coincides with a north–
south meridian line on the map. We look where it says "Read
Bearing Here" and we find that it says 320. Our map course is 320
degrees. Now we have to convert that reading to our magnetic
compass reading. Our declination is 10 degrees east. That means
our needle will be pointing 10 degrees farther east than true north.
So we have to subtract that from our 320 reading, giving us a compass bearing of 310. We set that on the dial. Now we use the
magnetic needle. With the needle lining up with "N", we sight
down the arrow from "Read Bearing Here," pick out a point on the

terrain and head for it.* By going from point to point, maintaining that 310 degrees compass bearing, we will hit Lake B right on the nose, if we can keep going straight.

Rough Terrain

It is not always possible to travel in a straight line through the woods, since cliffs and other features of the terrain interfere. To get around an impassable point, we may have to move to the left or right. Let us say we move 200 yards right. We stay on our 310 course, travelling parallel to our original route, but keeping in mind that we are 200 yards to the right. Once we clear the obstacle, we may be able to move back 200 yards to the left and thus pick up our original line. In the course of travel, we may move off our bearing by various distances to the right or left. We try to estimate those distances as accurately as possible and keep our new course parallel to our original one, so that we can later adjust and get back on course. If we have a prominent landmark to shoot for it is much easier. If Lake B happens to be a large body of ice we don't have to worry. We will merely hit the shore at whatever distance to the right or left we have been forced to move off our original 310 course. Obviously, distance estimating can lead to error. So we keep referring to our map, looking for recognizable landmarks and adjusting as we go.

Reading from Land Back to Map

Let us say that we are not exactly sure where we are but we can see a big hill off to the east. This is identified by the elevation on our contour map. We have been skirting a steep bluff along the edge of a drifted-in meadow and we would like to know just where the heck we are on that bluff. We aim our bearing arrow at the hill and rotate the compass until "N" and the needle line up. At "Read Bearing Here" we see that the hill has a magnetic bearing of 65 from where we stand. But we have that 10-degree declination to worry about. Now in this case we are going from the compass back to true north, which will be 10 degrees west of our compass reading. We have to *add* 10 degrees. Now we return to the map and draw a line at 75 degrees from the hill to the bluff. Where that line

Silva and others put out orienteering publications which explain compass work in detail. These are available at camping equipment stores.

hits the bluff on the map is where we are standing. We can locate this spot by other map features such as the edge of the meadow, a change in the contour of the bluff, a stream or another nearby hill. It is nice if there are two prominent hills or terrain features that can be sighted, since the point where the lines cross on the map will give an exact location. However, in much of the timbered country of the North, it is enough just to locate one good identifiable terrain feature.

To the uninitiated, all of this compass discussion may sound like a lot of gibberish. But it must be learned. It can be learned in a familiar neighborhood on day trips, where terrain features such as crossroads, schools, churches (steeples make nice check points), farms and bridges are easy to identify. By shooting compass lines to and from these easy-to-see landmarks and applying them to bearings, one can quickly learn the system. The wilderness at 40 below zero is no place for this kind of school.

Lensatic Compass

So far we have been working with a Silva compass with a plastic edge. The lensatic compass has no such feature, but it employs a lens and rifle-like sighting device for taking accurate field bearings. First our line is drawn on the map with some sort of a straight edge (map case, protractor) from known point A to Lake B. We center the compass where this line crosses a map meridian line and rotate the whole map until our compass needle lines up with 360 or north. Now we read where the meridian line passes under our compass and we get a 320 reading. We apply our 10-degree declination and come up with the 310-degree compass bearing. Holding the compass flat in one hand we sight down 310, line up the front and back sight on the compass with a prominent tree or some other distant terrain feature, fold up the compass, and head for it. When we get to our landmark, we shoot another line to some other distant landmark on the 310 bearing and continue over to Lake B.

Compass Problems

A compass can register wrong. This can happen if some iron object such as a knife or ice chisel is close by and attracts the needle. It can sometimes go haywire in the North where there are iron deposits in the ground . . . which is something to check locally

The author and partner check their map on an outing in the Boundary Waters Canoe Area, Minnesota.

prior to the trip. If the presence of iron is suspected, we usually move another two or three hundred yards and take another reading. In nearly all cases, it is not the compass playing tricks but that little direction finder inside the human head. Anyone who travels the woods a lot soon discovers that the mind tells a lot of lies when it comes to direction. This is why we carry compasses.

TRAIL HAZARDS

While snow is a great material to travel on, it also hides a good many booby traps. An established, packed trail is as safe as a sidewalk, but when you are breaking trail, there are some pitfalls to watch out for.

Bad Ice

Crossing rivers and lakes can get spooky if the traveller does not know how much ice lies beneath the snow. Narrow points of streams where the current speeds up may have treacherous ice. Any stream with a drop of five feet or more to the mile can be real trouble. Lakes have bad ice where streams enter and leave, around spring holes, and adjacent to beaver lodges and muskrat houses.

90

To test ice, it may be necessary to have one party member move slowly ahead, chipping regularly with the ice chisel to check thickness. When travelling unknown ice, we stay next to the shore where possible. If we have to cross an open area, we take a pole fifteen to twenty feet long and balance it under one arm. If we do fall through, the pole will catch on the edges of the ice and we will be able to scramble out. Also, a team can rope together crossing an open area so that anyone falling through can be pulled out by his comrades.

Reading Ice

Good ice, that which will give good support, is generally termed "blue" ice because it has that cast. The veteran winter traveller can kick snow off an area and often determine ice quality just by looking at it. It is sometimes possible to tell where there is poor ice under the snow by looking at the snow cover. It may have a grayish look or wet spots, or there may be depressed areas indicating a recent freeze. If there is open water nearby with wisps of vapor rising into the air, it is a good bet that the ice around the opening is poor. Late in the winter, just before breakup, ice will turn grainy and will darken, eventually turning blackish. This black or "rotten" ice has little or no support even though it may be a foot or more thick. Thin ice on streams can sometimes be detected by listening for moving water gurgling below.

Slush

This is a real problem in the North and has little to do with thin ice. Slush forms when a heavy snowfall weighs down the ice cover, forcing water to seep up through cracks from below. It can happen with two feet or more of ice on a lake. The slush may be six to eighteen inches thick. It forms an unfrozen layer between the ice and the surface snow. At 30 below zero, slush may lie in pockets for days without freezing. The first indication of slush the skier or snowshoer has is usually when water appears in his tracks or where his ski poles poke in. And he immediately stops. If the slush is just starting to form and is not deep, there may be no problem going over the top of it. But if it is already deep, the traveller will probably sink into it over his boot tops. On a warm day this means he will get a couple of wet feet while he is getting turned around and

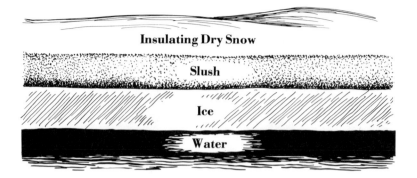

Insulating Dry Snow

Slush

Ice

Water

Dangerous slush can form just above ice after a snow.

out. On a bitter cold day he will have to stamp out of the slush with wet skis or snowshoes that immediately turn into two unmanageable twenty-pound globs of ice and snow. Furthermore, the whole mess will fuse with his boots so that he can't free the bindings. The veteran winter traveller who plows into slush gets out of his bindings quickly and gets into the woods where he can build a fire, thaw the ice off his skis or snowshoes and dry out his boots. And he does it pronto. If it means making camp right there, so be it. The alternative is frozen feet.

Blizzards

When a blizzard hits it can wipe out all landmarks. If the trail is well marked it may be possible to reach the next campsite. If not, the first possible camping area that appears should be used. It does not pay to wander in unfamiliar country in a blizzard. The chance of going over a bluff or through a hole in the ice is too great. Most blizzards involve a warming trend and heavy flakes, but a cold day with a wind and fine, blowing snow, may make it just as hard to see. The same can be true of winter fog. In a sentence: If you can't see, stop.

Wind-Chill

Quite a bit has been written about the "wind-chill factor," and there are a good number of charts available showing how it is computed, but only when a person gets involved in a cold and windy situation does he really appreciate it. One of the last times I got into a jam, my friend Mike Banovetz and I were ice fishing on a bitter January day. Just as we were starting for home we got into slush. With boots and pants freezing fast, we had the choice of building a big fire or heading for my warm cabin a half hour away. We chose the cabin and started in. The thermometer read 35 below, and the wind was gusting between fifteen and twenty-five miles per hour, which put the wind-chill equivalent between minus 80 and minus 95 degrees. We had no feeling in our feet and hands when we stumbled through the door . . . but that feeling came back a few painful moments later as the stove thawed our limbs. We howled and hopped around the room in what is known in the North Country as the "hurt dance." Fortunately, we had no permanent problems, although in another hour out there we could have frozen something.

The cooling power of wind added to cold temperatures is an erratic phenomenon. The most abrupt drop comes over the first five to fifteen miles per hour, which is what is usually encountered. Here is a wind-chill chart we use for winter work.

Wind Speed	Temperature (°F)															
Calm	40	35	30	25	20	15	10	5	0	-5	-10	-15	-20	-25	-30	-35
Equivalent Wind Chill																
5	35	30	25	20	15	10	5	0	-5	-10	-15	-20	-25	-30	-35	-40
10	30	20	15	10	5	0	-10	-15	-20	-25	-35	-40	-45	-50	-60	-65
15	25	15	10	0	-5	-10	-20	-25	-30	-40	-45	-50	-60	-65	-70	-80
20	20	10	5	0	-10	-15	-25	-30	-35	-45	-50	-60	-65	-75	-80	-85
25	15	10	0	-5	-15	-20	-30	-35	-45	-50	-60	-65	-75	-80	-90	-95
30	10	5	0	-10	-20	-25	-30	-40	-50	-55	-65	-70	-80	-85	-95	-100
35	10	5	-5	-10	-20	-30	-35	-40	-50	-60	-65	-75	-80	-90	-100	-105
40	10	0	-5	-15	-20	-30	-35	-45	-55	-60	-70	-75	-85	-95	-100	-110

Wind-Chill Table. Read the apparent temperature resulting from wind-chill where Wind Speed and Temperature lines intersect.

9: Meals and Nutrition

The key to outdoor eating in the winter is: "Keep the meals simple and serve everything possible hot." The gourmet summer camp cook may feel his style cramped in sub-zero temperatures. Not that the food can't be tasty . . . it's just that time and fuel cannot be wasted fussing over it.

COOKING UTENSILS AND EQUIPMENT

Griddles, reflector ovens, tin plates, frying pans and intricate nesting cook kits are best left home in the winter. All that is necessary are two pots for heating water and one bowl, cup and spoon for each member of the party. The two pots, one four-quart and one two-quart, provide an adequate source of hot water (a number 10 can with a wire handle will work as a pot). For quick, hot tea water using minimal fuel, European-style teapots like the flat, low, two-handled models made by Mountain Paraphernalia are excellent.

Other than the metal Sierra Club cup which maintains a cool rim, we avoid metal tableware because it will either burn the mouth or cool the food too quickly. Plastic bowls and cups of the dishwasher-safe variety, which will not lose their shape in hot water, are preferred, and some campers lean toward insulated plastic mugs. Everything served on a camping trip can be eaten with a spoon. Everyone keeps track of his own utensils.

Dishwashing in camp is simple. Spoons, bowls and cups can be cleaned out by adding a little hot water and wiping them out with a bit of paper towel which can be burned in the fire. Sometimes we simply take a couple of handfuls of snow to rub the insides of the cups and bowls and wipe off the spoons. In the cold, there is no problem with bacteria growing on any tiny particles of food left stuck to the tableware. Soap is not necessary for winter dishwashing. We avoid it because any trace of soap not properly rinsed from a bowl or cup will cause sickness and diarrhea, and rinsing in the cold may be difficult.

Frying is avoided. There is no greater mess in zero weather than attempting to clean up cooking gear caked with frozen grease. Frying takes too long and consumes too much fuel. Any baking needed is done before the trip. Baking with a reflector oven in the winter requires a lot of wood to produce the nice, even heat required. Moreover, it may be impossible to mix the dough without having it freeze.

TYPES OF MEALS

There are three main types of foods consumed on the trail: those made with hot water, those which can be thawed out next to an open fire, and those that can be eaten as is. We use all three on an average trip.

Hot Water Meals

The essential for this type of meal is a supply of pure water. This can be obtained from a hole cut in a lake or river (if the source is known to be good), from ice or from snow. Ice can be found against rock ledges where snow has melted and frozen. Ice from lakes or streams is no more pure than the source it comes from. Snow is a readily available source of water, but melting it requires time since it is seventeen parts air to one part water, as we mentioned in Chapter III. Simply adding snow to a hot pan for melting does not work well and may result in a scorched pan. The best method is to put some water in the pan first and add snow to the heating water. If this is not possible, the pan is warmed until sufficient snow has melted to provide a water base and then the heat is turned up.

A basic camp cooking setup is a pot of water on a single-burner pressure camp stove such as the Optimus 111B or Coleman Peak 1. Gravity stoves fizzle in extreme cold. Stoves should never be filled more than two-thirds full in the winter or they may leak fuel and cause a fire.

The hot water from this setup provides all necessary drinks: instant coffee, tea, bouillon, chocolate, Tang, hot Jello, punch or Russian tea. Some of these contain sugar for energy. Hot water creates the medium for such basics as instant, precooked rice (Minute Rice is good) and instant potatoes to go with canned, frozen or foil-pouch, precooked meats.

The new Retort foods, ready-to-eat main meat dishes, are just

now coming on the market. We have tested some of these tasty, foil-packed items, including beef and onions, beef loaf, smoked ham patties, chicken loaf and frankfurters. Although fairly expensive at present, these represent a breakthrough in light-weight, individually portioned meats for the camper.

Hot water is also the base for instant soups. We use the Lipton's Cup o' Soup in individual packets, sticking to the thick varieties such as pea, bean and cream of tomato. For breakfast we use hot water with instant Quaker Oats or Cream of Wheat in individual packets, sometimes combined with raisins or stewed fruit. Individual packets cost a little more than bulk soups or cereal but there are no leftovers and no sticky pots to clean. Homemade granola, which requires only the addition of water and powdered milk, is a nourishing breakfast and easy to handle.

When we have cereal, we line up the boxes of packets, sugar or stewed fruit, dry milk and butter on the bottom of a turned-over cross-country sled. All of the ingredients are dumped in the cup or bowl, then boiling water is added and the cereal stirred slightly. This may not sound exceptionally mouth-watering, but in the cold, everything tastes good.

Some nutritionists feel that refined sugar is not the great source of energy it was once thought to be, and that it has more drawbacks than advantages. We tend to lean toward fruit as a cereal sweetener.

Many topnotch camping food companies specialize in freeze-dried meal items that require no cooking, just the addition of boil-

Winter camp kitchen: stove, pots, bowls, cups and spoons.

ing water. The foods come in plastic or foil pouches and the instructions call for adding the hot water to the pouch and then letting the pouch stand for five minutes or so until the food reconstitutes. This works pretty well in the summer, but in the winter the pouches chill down too quickly and the foods do not reconstitute quickly. They come out tough and chewy. The same thing will happen if the foods are poured in a bowl and hot water added. Putting the correct amount of water in the cook pot, bringing it to a boil, and then adding the food and cutting the heat back on the stove will work. It is also possible to add hot water to the plastic food pouch and then set the pouch inside the hot water pot until the food reconstitutes. This way, it is possible to taste the item occasionally to determine when it is ready, and then take it from the heat.

Camping specialty stores carry a variety of these reconstituted trail foods. Two we have used extensively are RichMoor and Mountain House. Both are tasty and filling. Their no-cook main dishes include such items as beef stew, chicken stew, vegetable stew, turkey and noodles, beef and noodles, spaghetti, chicken and rice, beef and rice, chili, beans and franks, beef and potatoes, macaroni and cheese, chicken à la king and scrambled eggs. They also put out some excellent dessert items such as fruit cocktail and applesauce. In the summer we use their puddings, fruit cobblers and pineapple cheesecake mix, but in the winter we avoid these because of sticky pot problems. Instead, we lean to dried peaches, apricots, apple slices, banana slices, fruit bars, chocolate bars and cookies that can be eaten as is.

Thawed Frozen Foods

Winter allows the budget-minded camper the opportunity to prepare an unlimited assortment of main meal items or even whole dinners ahead of time, freeze them at home and thaw them out as needed on the trail. Casserole dishes such as macaroni and cheese, chili mac, tuna and mushroom, and turkey and noodles can be bagged in individual or two-man servings and frozen. Bean dishes, including chili, and a variety of stews can be laid out on a shallow baking tin, frozen up into chunks and sealed in plastic bags. Leftovers lend themselves nicely to conversion to bagged and frozen trail items. Cooked main meals, such as cube steaks, hamburgers,

Spam, fish patties or boned chicken can be put together with vegetables in individual servings, perhaps with a slice of bacon and a little onion, and rolled up in foil packets. We tend to lean toward individual servings of packaged, frozen items because it is easier to plan for any number of persons and also because they thaw and heat more quickly than larger units.

The plastic-bag foods can be thawed by placing the bag inside the hot water pot. Foil items thaw nicely placed on the coals of an open fire and heated until steam starts coming out from inside. Also included in our precooked units are several bannock wrapped in foil and sometimes even biscuits or cornbread. These keep fine when frozen and warmed on the coals of an open fire or propped up adjacent to the flames to reflect the heat. Cornbread has a tendency to crumble, but its flavor does not diminish. If frozen store bread is used, it should be removed from the plastic wrapper before thawing. The thin plastic used will melt from the heat of the fire long before the ice thaws from the loaf. Single slices toasted on a stick over the fire require the least time. Wieners and polish sausages can be thawed out by the fire, impaled on sticks and roasted. Again, it is best to remove the plastic cover from these when thawing them, since the fire will tend to melt it. Most of the foil-wrapped items can be eaten right out of the package, which saves cleaning pots or bowls. The only drawback to these home-cooked frozen dishes is that they contain water and add weight to the trip. However, since all the food is carried on the sled, the problem is less significant than it would be backpacking, and the party rapidly eats its way through the weight as each day passes.

COOKING ON THE FIRE

About the only actual cooking we do on a trip comes when we have steaks or fish. Sometimes we take fresh T-bone steaks to broil on the fire the first night out. We eat them with our fingers.

Fish chowder is made from freshly caught fish, preferably trout, which are filleted and cut into inch squares. If we have plenty of fuel, we cook it on the stove. If not, it goes on the fire. The cook pot is given a coat of soap on the outside so that the soot can be removed more easily later. To "lay in" the chowder, we put down a thin layer of diced onion and bacon (in the ratio of four strips of bacon to one large onion), made up at home before the trip. Then

we add a layer of fish, a layer of dehydrated potatoes au gratin, more onion, fish, etc., until it is all used up. The fish layers are well seasoned with salt and pepper. With the ingredients in place, water is added to the pot until it comes just to the top of the last layer. The mixture is brought to a boil, then set back to the edge of the fire, covered and allowed to simmer for forty minutes. A cup of dry milk and a square of butter are stirred in gently and the chowder is ready. This is a nourishing meal but it has the drawback of requiring that someone wash the pot, not a fun thing in the cold.

Another way to handle fish is to bake them in foil. A simple way is to gill and gut them, cut off the head and tail and then slice the fish in half up the backbone. This provides two half-pieces which cook through quicker than a whole fish. The half is laid in a foil square, skin down, then salted and two slices of bacon are laid over the top. The foil is then folded over to make a sealed pouch and the pouch placed on the coals. As the bacon cooks inside, it furnishes grease to keep the fish from burning or sticking to the foil, and it adds a little flavor, too. Put up in individual servings, the fish can be eaten right out of the packet.

The concession we make to cooking fish in the winter is mainly because the fish are already out there and available. We always feel it is a little silly to be camped alongside an excellent source of

100   9: *Meals and Nutrition*

tasty protein and not make use of it. Any leftover fish can be saved for lunch the next day.

It is noticeable that we use considerable foil in winter cooking, and this may be some cause for concern among backpackers who detest the aluminum "hatch" that occurs each summer around frequently used campsites. There is no question that foil must be eliminated from the campsite. Usually we fold it up and tuck it in the bottom of the food box for packing out. If we have a hot drying fire going, we sometimes spread the foil out in a single layer. It will oxydize over the flames in a couple of minutes. But we do not leave any trace at the campsite.

READY-TO-EAT FOODS FOR SNACKING

Topping this list are the pocket items for nibbling on during the day, including "gorp" made up of peanuts, small candies like M&M's, and maybe a few raisins or pieces of chopped dried fruit. Hard candies make good trail nibblers, and so do energy bars. We make the latter by stirring together 2 cups of white sugar, 2 cups of margarine, 1/3 cup of honey and 1/3 cup of corn syrup until they are creamy smooth, then adding 9½ cups of rolled oats and 1 cup of sliced almonds. The mix is spread on a greased 9-by-13-inch cookie tin and baked for about 18 minutes in a 350-degree oven until it is golden brown. It is cut into squares and folded into foil wrappers.

Fruitcake is one of the foods highest in energy and was a staple with many arctic expeditions. Homemade cookies are good nibblers and so are dried fruits, such as apples and apricots, along with fruit bars and jerky.

LUNCH ITEMS

Cheese, jam, honey, canned meat, peanut butter, dry sausage, braunschweiger and any number of freeze-dried trail lunches will work fine at midday, especially when combined with a hot drink or hot instant soup. Some of these items, however, will freeze hard and may be difficult to serve unless someone has planned ahead. A can of Spam can be dropped in the pot to thaw while the tea water is being heated. Sausage can be sliced the night before and put up in individual packets to be carried in the inside shirt pocket during the day so that it will be thawed and ready at lunchtime. Cheese can be purchased already sliced at the supermarket and the packet carried inside a pocket where it will not freeze hard. Peanut butter, jam and honey should be removed from glass jars and put up in plastic containers which will not break if their contents freeze. If the ingredients are stiff and unmanageable, the jars can be placed in the pot while the beverage water is heating. Sausage can be loosened up in the same way, although a thawing salami does not appreciably add to the flavor of hot tea water. The trail food makers put out a lot of water-mix lunch packets, including chicken salad, tuna salad and cheese spread. These need only the addition of cool water, not hot, to reconstitute, and they are very tasty.

Since loaves of bread are difficult to thaw, we use crackers like GI hardtack or Ritz with our lunches. For bread, we prefer bannock baked at home, frozen in foil and packed one for each meal. There are innumerable recipes for bannock. Here is a simple one: Mix together 3 cups of flour, a level tablespoon of baking powder, 4 heaping tablespoons of brown sugar, a teaspoon of salt, ½ cup raisins and ⅔ cup of dehydrated milk. Stir in 2 tablespoons of vegetable oil and then add enough water (about a cup) to knead into a pliable, rubbery dough. Smooth it into a disc about 10 inches across and place in a greased frying pan and bake at 350 degrees until brown and crisp on top. Each bannock is wrapped in foil and frozen. At supper time, it is propped up next to the open fire or laid in the coals and heated. At lunch time, it is used as the pot cover and heated with the water until it can be sliced or broken apart.

SEASONING

We carry salt and pepper. Ample salt is as necessary as water to replace that lost in perspiration. However, excess salt will tend to dry out the lips, which are probably already dry enough, and cracked or split lips in the winter are no source of joy. Some campers carry a little kit of spices to doctor up the flavor of trail foods. Bottled items like ketchup or mustard are useless since they will freeze and break.

CALORIES

The name of the game is heat. High-calorie foods are heat producers and keep the human machine operating in the cold. Canadian

Army specialists note that the energy the body consumes travelling on the snow trail, combined with the need to produce body heat, requires consuming almost twice the normal amount of food. Depending on the individual (some people have a greater cold tolerance) it takes between 4,000 and 5,000 calories per day to maintain a warm, operating body. Quick energy comes from sugar, which is why we nibble gorp, candy and fruit frequently en route. Energy-producing fats are found in vegetable derivatives including peanut butter, margarine, butter and cheese as well as in meat items.

It has been our experience that people who prefer all-vegetable diets sometimes have difficulty keeping warm in sub-zero situations. I do not wish to get into any debate on this, but the Inuit, who spend their lives in the arctic, are essentially meat and animal fat eaters. They do not thrive on berries and roots. On the trail, they eat a lot of raw meat such as caribou. Through trial and error, the Inuit discovered that by eating raw meat they avoided sickness. They did not know that the reason for this was that the Vitamin C that exists in raw meat is removed by boiling. Without citrus fruits or other sources of Vitamin C, they had to rely on raw meat for their supply. Some early arctic explorers, among them members of the tragic Franklin Expedition, died of scurvy on a diet of boiled meat because they did not understand the importance of eating the meat uncooked.

High-protein foods are fuel producers. Thus, cheese, peanuts, fruitcake, beef, pork and fish, which are high in calorie count, are also high in protein count. Prior to turning in at night, we eat something high in protein which will keep on producing heat while we sleep. Also, to conserve as much energy as possible, we get well warmed by the fire just before crawling into the sleeping bag. Although energy consumption drops during sleep, just the act of breathing requires a lot of calories to warm up the air in the throat before it enters the lungs.

LIQUIDS

In winter, the human body uses up something like two quarts of water each day, as mentioned in Chapter VII. Breathing alone releases a lot of moisture from the body. Perspiration releases more. Water must be continually replaced or dehydration will set in causing serious problems with body metabolism and resultant loss of heat and energy. The first thing in the morning, we have a pot of hot water going so that each member of the party can have a hot drink just before and with breakfast.

We fill our individual flasks with water after breakfast and sip on these during rest stops, replacing consumed water with snow or refilling from a spring hole or riffle if the water supply in the area is pure. As we mentioned in Chapter VI, we do not drink directly from the cold water source, although that water may be very refreshing in the winter. Instead, the water goes into the plastic neck bottle where it will be warmed somewhat by the body. When we drink it, it will be lukewarm and not nearly as tasty as that open spring hole, but it will cause no heat loss when it hits the stomach.

Again, at lunch, we have two or three cups of beverage and then refill our neck bottles with the leftover warm water. Liquid intake is limited to the period of time between breakfast and supper. Late evening snacks consist only of solids. Otherwise the "bladder alarm clock" is likely to make sleep impossible after 4 A.M., which is an uncomfortable time to tiptoe out of the tent at 30 below. The formula is:

> During the day drink lots of water;
> After supper you hadn't ought'er.

10: Winter First Aid

If I were looking for odds, I would suspect that there is far less real danger, hour for hour, on a sub-zero camping trip than there is in driving the family car in the summer. This does not mean that accidents cannot happen on the trail. They can. But just as the auto safety experts advise people to "drive defensively," so the snow traveller on foot uses his eyes and mind to continually assess the situation, anticipating possible problems.

If a mishap does occur on a camping trip or in any other situation, most first aid teachers propose this procedure: (1) Assess the situation; (2) form a plan; (3) follow the plan. In order to do this with any intelligence, you need a knowledge of first aid. There is no substitute for Red Cross or some similar type of training by skilled instructors. Every city in the U.S. has first aid training available through its Red Cross, its school system or both. This is worthwhile knowledge not only for campers, but at home, on the job or on the highway. You can bet your life on it.

For simplicity, we have divided the common trail emergencies into two categories: Those that can be handled by the group and those that require outside help. First Aid is just that. Unless a member of the party is a licensed physician, no involved treatment is attempted.

PROBLEMS THE GROUP CAN HANDLE

These are common occurrences on the trail and do not ordinarily abort the trip, although if they are severe enough or if complications set in, they could. In any event, the group can handle the problem, whether it requires treatment on the spot or packing out the injured party.

Frostbite

In frostbite some portion of the human anatomy is frozen. Most often this happens to the exposed parts of the face: nose, cheeks, ears, neck. The symptoms are white or yellow-white patches appearing on the skin. Face freezing most often occurs in cold, windy situations. Because it is preceded by numbness in the affected part, the victim may not be aware of his problem. For this reason we continually stop on the trail to check each other for frostbite. The treatment for minor freezing of the face is to get out of the wind and place a warm, bare hand on the affected spot until the color returns. The spot is not rubbed (which can damage tissue) but just covered with the hand. The victim can do this himself or he can alternate with somebody else as their hands get cold. Care must be taken to see that the face does not freeze up all over again. Frostbite on the face can usually be prevented by the use of a face mask and/or muffler along with a cap and parka hood. It is a recognized fact that any area of the body which has just been frostbitten will re-freeze more quickly than healthy tissue.

Other common areas for frostbite are the fingers, hands and feet. Hands become stiff and numb. When the mitten is removed, the fingers are white. The quickest way to thaw them is to shove them up inside the parka under the armpits. It is obvious that warm armpits do not readily accept this accommodation with icy bare hands, but accept it they must. Feet are a real frostbite problem. There is no easy way for the victim to get his feet up under his armpits. Two warm hands placed over the affected part will help. The trouble with feet is that they have to be removed from the boots which further exposes them and can make the frostbite worse. The recommended thawing procedure is to place the cold, bare feet inside the parka against the warm tummy of a companion. (This is when you find out who your friends really are.)

If the situation warrants, it may be necessary to stop and build a fire in a sheltered spot. The frostbitten area should be identified and the problem offset as much as possible with cover and insulation. The other alternative is to get out of the weather by making camp.

There is another type of frostbite that comes from grabbing metal items with bare hands. While this usually results in an immediate sensation like a burn, it may not if the hands are numb. There have been some painful injuries to people who attempted to use an ice spud with bare hands in below-zero conditions, or grabbed a metal lantern, stove or saw blade. Even with knit gloves it does not pay to hold a frigid metal object for more than a few

10: Winter First Aid

moments. Such an injury has the same effect as a burn and it will usually blister. About the only treatment is to keep the injury clean and covered with a clean bandage.

Sprains

These are usually ankle injuries, but they could also affect the wrist, fingers, or knee. They result from a twisting or stretching of a joint, damaging ligaments, tendons and blood vessels. They occur mostly in spills on hills when somebody gets tangled up in his skis or snowshoes. A sprain is a painful injury accompanied by swelling and a lack of strength at the injured joint. It is sometimes difficult to distinguish from a fracture because of swelling. However, the fracture victim usually has a good idea what happened because he heard a distinct "pop" when the bone broke, and usually there is some sort of deformity, although this may not be true of a chip fracture.

A sprained limb must be immobilized to prevent further damage. And this can present some first-class problems, especially if the ankle or knee is involved. If it is possible and a site is nearby, camp can be pitched. If the accident occurs some distance from a good site, it may be possible to immobilize an ankle with an Ace or Coban bandage on the outside of the boot. Even a section of nylon line can be used to lock the foot in place. The limb will still hurt, but the victim may be able to shuffle to camp if the rest of the gang takes his pack or sled. The alternative is to put him in the sled and skid him to camp.

An ankle sprain will swell inside the boot, reduce circulation and invite frostbite. On the other hand, if the boot is removed, swelling may make it impossible to get it back on. That is why we try to immobilize the limb with the boot on until we get to a campsite. Then the boot can be removed and the swelling reduced somewhat by packing the limb with snow for a few minutes, taking care to prevent any possible freezing. Between brief applications of snow, the limb should be kept covered and warm.

With a wrist or elbow sprain, snow can be applied right away to reduce swelling and then the limb can be immobilized with a bandage over the outside of the parka until camp is reached. While not as disabling as an ankle sprain, an arm injury does not improve poling technique. After the sprain has been treated in camp, an

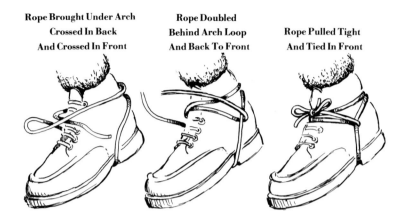

Rope Brought Under Arch Crossed In Back And Crossed In Front

Rope Doubled Behind Arch Loop And Back To Front

Rope Pulled Tight And Tied In Front

Use of rope to immobilize sprained ankle.

elastic bandage will hold the limb immobile and still allow for swelling. Adhesive tape is not used since it can cut circulation and cause freezing. With a minor sprain, the victim may be able to travel within eighteen to twenty-four hours.

As a general rule with a sprain on the trail, the elastic bandage goes over the outside clothing. After the party has reached camp and the swelling has been arrested, the elastic bandage can go over the limb under the clothing.

Minor Burns

These usually result from grabbing a hot lantern, stove or pot. If the fingers are cold the burn can become severe before the hand gets the message. Burns can also result from clothing catching on fire while a camper is wearing it by the fire to dry out, from synthetics "melting" against the skin and from fire caused by smoking in the sleeping bag, among other things. A very common and sometimes quite painful burn occurs to the feet when some soggy trail pusher gets his boots near the fire to "dry them off." Usually this is done by sitting down, soles to the flames. The heat starts

10: Winter First Aid

through the bottom of the boot, and by the time it reaches the foot and the nerve ends tell the camper he is in trouble, the heat is continuing to build up in the composition sole and the camper has given himself a wholesale hotfoot. Not only is this a ridiculous way to dry out boots, but it is also a good way to burn off the bottoms.

The first thing to do to a burn is to stop the heat by plunging the affected part into the snow. Carefully dry it. The injury is then covered by a dry sterile bandage. Butter, lard or ointment does little for a burn except make it greasy. Blisters are not "popped." If they happen to break, they are kept covered by a sterile dressing to prevent infection.

Cuts

These usually happen to the hands when working with a knife, although they can be caused by handling the edges of metal containers or opening tin cans. A minor cut can be closed with a band-aid. A more severe cut may require several butterfly closures and a sterile bandage. First aid must be quick and sure, not allowing any excessive exposure of the injured part to the cold.

Since we do not carry an axe, we avoid axe cuts, which can be very severe. The sharp end of an ice chisel left lying around with the sheath off can cause a leg or ankle cut. Ski pole tips can cause puncture wounds. These usually occur when two people, running too close together, pile up on a hill. Punctures are "bad" wounds since foreign material is often driven into the injury and bleeding is not sufficient to clean it. The wound should be cleaned, if possible, with warm water and soap, then covered with a sterile bandage. The bandage should be changed regularly and any signs of infection noted. A severe puncture automatically signals the end of the trip and a visit to the doctor.

Eye Injuries

Getting whipped in the face with a rebounding branch is a common cause of eye injuries in timber country. Keeping a wide interval between skiers or snowshoers prevents this. While painful, such injuries are seldom serious. Snow blindness is another potential hazard, particularly late in the winter when there is more sunlight and the snow surface reflects light. Dark glasses or goggles prevent this affliction. The symptoms of snow blindness are similar to those experienced when you get a flash in the eye from an electric welding torch. The eyes burn, feel gritty, water, and may swell shut. Further exposure to light must cease. Application to the eyes of a cold compress for a few minutes may help. The eyes should be covered with a clean bandage and the patient kept out of the bright sunlight. Obviously further travel is not possible until the situation clears up.

In the winter there is little likelihood of getting bits of dirt or sand in your eye, but it is possible to get a bit of bark in it when pulling down branches for firewood. It is possible to locate such a particle on the lower lid by rolling the lid down, lashes first, with a wooden match. If spotted, the particle may be picked out with a bit of cotton or gauze. Watering of the eye will usually cause objects on the upper lid to work their way down. Anything stuck to the eyeball itself should not be touched until it moves to the inside of the lid. All eye injuries should be treated as serious, since any impairment of vision can cause a more serious injury. Only a doctor is qualified to handle cuts to the eye, objects embedded in the eye or other serious eye problems.

Allergies, Chronic Illness

People who have allergies or problems such as diabetes are not eliminated from winter camping unless their doctor forbids it. However, they must be certain that they have their medication along on the trip, and that other members of the group are aware of their condition and know what medication is required and where it is kept. If it is in liquid form, the medication should not be allowed to freeze.

We have a friend by the name of Pat Flanary who is an employee of the State Forestry Division and who is as tough an outdoorsman as they come. Pat suffers from chronic respiratory problems and is allergic to fish, peanut butter and fur . . . which is a pretty bad combination for anybody who likes to fish and hunt. But it doesn't stop him. He takes along his asthma medication, lets the rest of the gang handle his fish, avoids peanut butter and doesn't wear a parka with a fur collar. On the ski trails he wheezes along like a steam engine, but he pulls more than his share of the load, pitches in wholeheartedly with camp chores and makes it on sheer guts and desire. Having a physical handicap does not neces-

110   *10: Winter First Aid*

sarily stop anybody from winter camping just as long as they know how to handle their problem.

Asphyxia

This condition is most commonly caused by stove or lantern fumes inside the tent. Tests conducted on small, one-burner camping stoves show varying amounts of released gases, but all stoves are dangerous. Stoves or lanterns are used only for short periods inside the tent and then only where there is adequate cross-ventilation. The greatest hazard of asphyxiation is from carbon monoxide, which is odorless and invisible. Symptoms of carbon monoxide poisoning are drowsiness, headache, anxiety, stupor. The treatment is to open the tent up and shut off the stove or lantern. Get outside and pump fresh air into your lungs and bloodstream. It is worthwhile to read Rear Admiral Richard E. Byrd's account of his poisoning by fumes from a power generator while he was alone at an outpost in Antarctica. The generator was used to operate the radio that kept him in touch with base personnel nearer the coast. As his transmissions daily grew more erratic, other members of the expedition became concerned and pushed out to his rescue, arriving just as Byrd became entirely immobilized.

Head and Stomach Complaints

Constipation is a common winter problem, and while not usually serious in itself, it can cause stomach cramps and nausea. If time does not handle the problem, a laxative will. Headaches are common in winter travel due to many causes including dehydration, overexertion, eyestrain and bad food. Aspirin will help alleviate the symptoms, and an investigation of possible causes may end the problem. Diarrhea is a lesser problem for winter campers since food spoilage is minimal, unwashed utensils pose no problem and we do not get soap inside the cook pots. We have a minimum of sickness on winter trips, although occasionally somebody will get a bellyache from eating too much candy or perhaps not taking in enough liquids. I have a problem with hot chocolate, which I dearly love, but which will give me a first-class stomach upset if I drink more than two cups at a sitting. Eating snow can also cause stomach cramps. Snow must be melted into water before it is consumed.

Intestinal Problems   111

Windy →

← Cold

. Wet →

← Tired

This camper is in trouble: a classic hypothermia situation is in the making.

Hypothermia

Hypothermia is a condition in which heat loss from the body results in a temperature drop from which the body by itself cannot recover. This may or may not be extremely serious, depending on how far it develops, but it must be treated immediately on the trail. Symptoms of hypothermia are uncontrollable shivering, lack of coordination, slurred speech and exhaustion.

Once the body temperature drops a few degrees, physiological changes begin to take place over which the person has no control. The circulation to the extremities is curtailed and the body conserves the remaining warm blood supply around the heart and lungs, the vital organs. When this happens, fresh supplies of oxygen-rich blood to the brain are reduced and the victim cannot function normally. Hallucinations are common. Survivors of winter

10: Winter First Aid

tragedies have told our search-and-rescue people of seeing automobiles parked on the ice that vanished when they approached, hearing traffic on nonexistent highways, trying to start fires with imaginary matches, even making calls from pay phones that simply never existed. Obviously, in this state of mind it is almost impossible for the victim or victims to get a camp erected and a fire started.

Once hypothermia sets in, the body cannot recover by itself. The cooling process continues, resulting in stupor, convulsions and death. The process, if it has not progressed too far, can be reversed dramatically by the application of external and internal warmth. The winter traveller must be always alert to the conditions which could lead to hypothermia: wet clothing, wind and rapid cooling of the body. The problem is seldom caused by dry cold, even in subzero temperatures. It is more apt to happen at 40 degrees above zero on a windy, thawing day when the garments become wet.

The treatment for hypothermia is to get out of the wind, build a fire and erect a shelter. Get the victim's wet clothes off, put him inside a sleeping bag and have someone crawl in with him to produce body heat, or have two people crawl in with him in a double bag. If the victim is conscious, give him frequent sips of warm water, tea or coffee. When he begins to come out of it, get him into warm, dry clothing, keep him close to the fire and give him some high-energy food to nibble on.

Memorize the hypothermia danger signs: Wet, cold, wind, tiredness and prolonged shivering. Memorize the antidote: Stop, get out of the wind, build a fire, get warm and dry, drink something warm, eat.

Problems Requiring Outside Help

When a serious accident occurs or if a member of the party becomes sick and incapacitated, again we follow our three-point procedure: (1) Assessing the situation; (2) making the plan; and (3) following the plan.

When an incident occurs, the assessment is made in this order: (1) Is the patient breathing? If not, artificial respiration must be started immediately. (2) Is the heart beating? If there is no pulse or detectable heartbeat, cardiac massage should be started at once. This works best with two people alternating between mouth-to-mouth resuscitation and massage. (3) Is the patient bleeding? If so, bleeding must be stopped. Remember that bleeding may not be immediately visible under clothing. (4) What happened? If the victim is conscious, determine what occurred so that a rapid inspection of the injury can be made without exposing any more of the person to cold than is necessary. If the victim is not conscious, someone who witnessed the accident may be able to give an account. (5) Assume that shock either is or will be present. Shock is a drastic reaction of the body to trauma. It is associated with an impaired flow of blood. The symptoms are paleness, cold perspiration on the face, shallow breathing, weak pulse, blank staring eyes, nausea. The treatment is as follows: Keep the victim prone, but move him as little as possible. Place foam pads or sleeping bags under him and cover him lightly to keep him warm but not perspiring. Remember he is not moving and not generating his own heat. Provide lukewarm water to drink if the victim is fully conscious and has no abdominal injuries. If it is very cold, build a fire nearby. (6) Reassure the patient. It is essential that the injured person be kept as quiet and comfortable as possible, that he understand that he is in good hands, that procedure is under way to get medical help and that he is going to be okay. It is important that everyone on the scene have this calm, confident attitude. The patient is under enough stress already and he does not need somebody running around crying out about how badly he is hurt. Nor should relatives or close friends be allowed to cry or carry on within earshot. If he gets panicky, the patient can be pushed back into shock.

Fractures

Breaks in the bones of the ankle or leg incapacitate the victim for all further self-propelled travel. Breaks of the wrist or arm may allow a certain minimum of travel. The treatment is to immobilize the break to prevent further damage. If a simple break occurs (in which the bone does not break the skin), splint the injury *outside* the clothing, using plenty of padding. What do you use for splints? Some books show skis or ski poles used as splints. This is fine if you have extras, but if you don't, how does the party get out of the woods? One of the best splints is the cardboard box in the sled that the food is packed in. The bottom is cut out of the box and the

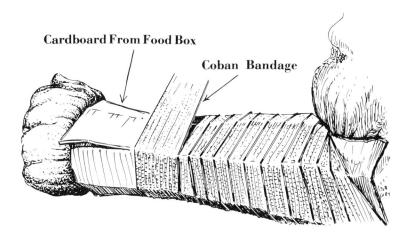

Cardboard From Food Box

Coban Bandage

To splint a fracture,
use materials at hand.

sides laid out to form one continual strip. This is rolled carefully around the break to form a cylinder, and taped in place. A section of Ensolite pad rolled into a cylinder will also make a splint. Of course, that pretty well finishes the pad. If the break is compound (the bone punctures the skin), carefully remove the clothing or slit it with a razor blade to determine if bleeding is occurring. Stop any bleeding, cover the fracture with gauze pads and splint it on the outside of the clothing. In the case of leg injuries, the broken leg can be splinted to the good leg with sufficient padding between, and the lower torso encased in a sleeping bag.

Dislocations

Dislocations occur when a bone of the arm or leg is wrenched out of its socket by either a fall or a strain. These injuries are very painful. They should be splinted or otherwise immobilized and the patient kept warm. Except for a minor dislocation such as a finger, no attempt to relocate the bone should be made by anyone other than a doctor. Even a finger is serious although I have had a couple yanked back in place by people other than an M.D. Again, wrap, bandage or tape the injury outside the clothing where possible.

Fractures   115

Severe Burns

These occur usually when the tent catches on fire or someone spills stove fuel on his clothing and it ignites. Severe burns can also result when somebody is trying to start a fire with stove fuel and a spark sets the can off. Shock is almost certain following such a burn. Clothing may be stuck to the wound. The treatment is to cover with a sterile pad or bandage. Do not try to remove burned cloth or skin. Do not rub on ointment. Keep the wound well covered and the patient immobile and warm.

Deep Cuts

Check for arterial bleeding, usually indicated by spurts of bright red blood. The blood is bright red because it is coming directly from the heart and is high in oxygen. It must be stopped quickly or the patient will die. Pressure is applied firmly right over the wound and also against any bone between the wound and the heart. A tourniquet is not used. A tourniquet will stop the flow of all blood, not just that in the artery, will kill tissue and can cause severe freezing. If the cut is not an arterial one, it may bleed a lot but it will not spurt. Any clothing or foreign material should be removed from the wound and then pressure applied directly until the bleeding ceases. As little of the body as possible should be exposed to the weather. When the bleeding has stopped, the wound can be dried, sealed up with a series of butterfly closures and covered with a bandage.

Heart Attack

While most winter sports enthusiasts stay in reasonably good condition, there is always the outside chance that a member of the group could have a cardiac emergency, or that the group could come upon some other campers with that problem. Most people are aware of the symptoms: Difficulty in breathing, chest pains, coughing, a bluish look around the lips, pain down the left arm and up the neck, nausea, paleness. What to do about it in the snow is something else. Generally it is best to get the patient prone and quiet with several foam pads under him and a sleeping bag laid lightly over. In no case can he be moved. In some instances, the pain may leave and the patient may decide he is just fine, get up and buy the farm. If he is short of breath, his head may be raised slightly. He should be kept calm, his suspected condition not discussed. Any stress or fright can cause death. Keep him comfortable. A fire should be built nearby and someone sent immediately for help.

Severe Freezing

If a part of the anatomy, such as the foot, becomes badly frostbitten, it will be white or yellow-white and hard, with an appearance like marble. It is like any other piece of frozen meat. Thawing it on the spot may not be the best move, since as long as the member is frozen there is little pain. A person can still function and get out of the woods on a frozen foot. Not so with a thawed-out frozen foot. Once a frozen limb begins to thaw it will swell, discolor, blister and become extremely painful. It will also quickly freeze again if not given immediate professional help. Medical treatment of frostbite has now advanced to the point that hospitals can save almost any hand or foot that comes in frozen. But if the member has been frozen, thawed and then refrozen, it will often have to be amputated. How to proceed with a case of severe freezing is a tough decision to make and depends on the situation and available help.

GETTING HELP FOR THE VICTIM

On a winter trip, the decision whether to move an emergency case out or to bring help in depends on where the party is and the type of injury that has occurred. A good knowledge of the area and of search-and-rescue procedure is invaluable.

Bringing Him Out

If the decision is made to bring the patient out to a road or to a frozen lake where ski plane rescue is possible, he can be bundled onto the cross-country sled and skidded along with one or more additional sled mules lashed into harness with extra lengths of rope. If the victim's legs are O.K., he may be able to shuffle along on his own power or with help alongside. He may not have any fun, but he'll be mobile.

While the move is under way to bring the injured camper out, one member of the party may be delegated to sprint to the nearest phone for help, to make sure that there is a vehicle waiting at the nearest access or that a plane will be brought into a designated lake or river. Whoever goes for help should have the following information written down: The name and address of the person bringing the message, name and address of the injured party, the extent of the injury, any treatment given, the exact location where the victim is or where he will be taken and the route being used to bring him out. This information should be given either in person or by telephone to someone in authority: A park or forest ranger, the state police, game warden, the search-and-rescue headquarters or the sheriff's police.

More than one call or contact should be made until the person making the call is sure that the rescue wheels are moving. Sometimes a person seeking help will meet other skiers, snowmobilers, hikers or motorists. While it is worthwhile to give them the message, it pays to keep on and contact more people. One of the most frustrating things that can happen to search-and-rescue personnel is to get a phone call from someone who reports that they met "a guy in trouble who has a friend injured out in the woods," and does not know where that injured person is. That is why each contact, where possible, should be written as a note that can be read over the phone or delivered in person. It may take several notes, but only one may get the job done.

In most winter camping areas there are organized search-and-rescue teams which can be called upon to head out via ski plane, snowmobile, snowshoe, ski or truck. Most of these teams operate with two-way radio contact and also are trained to alert doctors or hospitals if an emergency case is coming in. They are very efficient if they know where the patient is and what to expect when they get there.

Bringing Help In

If it is determined that the victim cannot be moved, someone must immediately be delegated to go for help. This is another reason for developing an intimate knowledge of an area, including roads, railroads, settlements, any place where help or communication is available. When contact is made with the authorities, an official

10: Winter First Aid

rescue mission will be mounted, probably with a doctor in the group.

In the meantime, camp is set up at the accident site, a fire is built and the victim is kept as warm and comfortable as possible. It must be kept in mind that his metabolism will be lowered from the injury, that he is immobilized and that he will probably not be producing normal body heat. He should be checked often and given warm water to drink if he is conscious. To make the best use of the fire, it may be necessary to erect a windbreak behind the patient. While this is being built, someone can stack up a supply of green material to be thrown on the fire for a smoke signal if an airplane or snowmobile motor is heard. Since few camping groups carry two-way radios, the people at the accident site may have little or no idea what method of rescue is being used. Thus it is well to be prepared for both air and ground assistance. If there is a lake, river or clearing nearby, the word HELP can be stamped out in the snow in huge letters and an arrow stamped out pointing toward the accident site. A blaze orange kitchen fly or tent fly can be staked out and is highly visible from the air. A bright jacket waved on a stick can be seen from a good distance. Most planes set up for rescue work have a bullhorn on board so that the pilot can call down and instruct the people on the ground what procedure will be followed.

Most rescue operations are accomplished by volunteers who use their own equipment and fuel. An offer by the rescued party to pay the expenses of the operation is certainly in order. It must be expected that any airplane flights and medical costs will be paid for by the rescued party.

Personal Winter First Aid Kit

There are a lot of compact first aid kits on the market, some of them fairly good, some not. We make up our own with the following items:

Two dozen band-aids in large and medium sizes	One 3-inch Coban bandage
	One 2-inch Coban bandage
A dozen Telfa pads, large and medium	Tweezers
	Scalpel in a sheath

Two dozen various-sized butterfly closures
One roll of 1-inch gauze bandage
One roll of 2-inch gauze bandage
Six 4-by-4 gauze pads
Two rolls of Dermicel tape
Four wooden tongue depressors (which double as finger splints)
One 2-inch Ace elastic bandage
Hemostat
Single-edged razor blade in a cardboard sheath
Aspirin
Laxative
One dozen large safety pins
A dozen kitchen matches in a container
A small, hotel-sized bar of soap
Six eye pads
Sunburn cream
Note paper and pencil

This is all carefully packed in a heavy gauge, bright-colored, plastic bag, rolled up tight and sealed with a couple of large rubber bands. Personal preference or local conditions may indicate additions or substitutions to the above.

Again, no matter how much equipment you carry, there is no substitute for training in a first aid class.

11: Activities around Camp

With the tent snugged down in a sheltered grove, the kitchen tarp slung and an adequate supply of dry wood stacked, it is time to take a day or more to relax, explore the country free of packs and sled and participate in winter's colorful ice show.

PHOTOGRAPHY

Every camping group wishes to record its adventures on film, and one or more of the members will probably have cameras. For good results it is sometimes prudent to have different film in each camera—that is, high-speed color in one, slower speed in another. That way, if light conditions or human error result in exposure problems in one camera, the other will pick up the story.

Camera and Film Care

In extreme cold there are a multitude of factors that can affect photo-taking. The most common problem is moisture inside the camera, which will cause the shutter to stick. Camera shops will "winterize" a unit for a fee. Some photographers dry their cameras in a warm oven for thirty minutes or more, keeping the oven door open. Taking a camera from room temperature into the cold is seldom a problem, but bringing it from the cold outdoors into a warm room or tent can cause a quick moisture buildup on the lens and metal parts. If the camera is cold, it is usually best to let it remain cold for the duration of the trip. Also, care must be taken while filming to direct your breath away from the viewing lens or it will fog up.

Films become brittle in the cold and require careful handling. If the film advance sticks, it should not be forced. After dark in a cold tent, the camera can be opened and the jam released or the partially used film rewound and a new one loaded.

Lighting

Shooting snow scenes offers some breathtaking color contrasts but it also can be frustrating. Good sunlight is nearly foolproof but overcast, cloudy days are very tricky and usually give very poor results except for closeups or flash pictures. Time exposure night scenes taken around the fire, stove or lantern offer some interesting effects.

NATURE STUDY

There is a tendency to consider the winter outdoor world buttoned down in hibernation, but in fact there is a good deal of activity going on, some of it much more evident than in the summer.

Reading Tracks

Fascinating tales are revealed through the tracks of deer, wolf, lynx, rabbit, squirrel, otter, fisher, moose, fox, weasel and other species. Many times we have tracked timber wolves, studying their tactics as they stalked a deer, sometimes successfully, sometimes not. Twice we have come upon battle grounds where rival wolf packs fought to the death over territory, the victors consuming the vanquished down to their hair. Near open riffles on streams, both otter and mink wade in and out of the water on fishing expeditions and in late winter muskrat and beaver can be observed perched on the rim of ice.

Bird Study

While many birds migrate to southern areas, some species remain in the north all winter long and a few arctic dwellers never move out of the snow zone. Ravens and some owls are cold weather residents along with tiny chickadees, blue and Canada jays and woodpeckers. "Ice ducks," the hardy goldeneye, are the last to move south and the first back when openings appear on the streams.

ICE FISHING

The area where we live, the Minnesota–Ontario border, is dotted with lakes, and it is a rare winter camping trip when we do not haul some short rods, tackle and a package of frozen minnows to

try for lake trout, walleyes or northern pike. Our goal in this endeavor is to acquire one or two fairly large fish which can be filleted, cut into squares and rendered into chowder, as discussed in Chapter IX. Through January and February, when trout are active, some of our expeditions are aimed at acquiring a supply of these silvery trophies for later gourmet dining at home. Along with frozen minnows, we carry a small box with hooks, sinkers, some marabou jigs and a few silver spoons.

Our rods are about thirty inches long; reels are level wind, loaded with ten-pound test monofilament. These take up little space and are packed with the ice chisel and ice skimmer in the sled.

There is no chance of fish spoiling in the winter. They can dry out in extreme cold, however. We bury our fish under a foot or more of snow, where they will stay cold but will not dehydrate, until we are ready to head home. Usually we bring the fish close to the fire to dress them, leaving the entrails on a stump for the ravens to feast on.

TREE STUDY

Outside of the pines, firs, spruce, cedars and hemlocks which retain their greenery all winter, trees in winter present a challenge to identification. Most deciduous trees are easy to name with the leaves in hand but with only bark and twigs for clues the situation is more of a test. There are some edible shrubs available to the informed. One of our favorites is Labrador tea, a spicy, aromatic shrub that grows thickly in spruce swamps, and can be easily located even in midwinter. We sometimes haul a bag of leaves home for later use. A paperback reference on trees and shrubs is a handy item to have along on a winter camping trip.

STAR STUDY

Clear winter nights are unparalleled for observing the heavens. The stars appear as glittering crystals on a black backdrop, the moon a great, glowing ball of pale opaque glass. On bright nights, when there is adequate surface, we sometimes spend an hour or two of invigorating moonlit skiing or snowshoeing through the frozen silence—taking care, of course, to keep oriented in regard to the location of camp.

COLD WEATHER SKETCHING

The artist, professional or amateur, can never in a studio duplicate the subject matter, composition and color encountered outdoors. Cold, however, limits the artist's medium as well as his method, since ink or watercolors will quickly freeze and so will unprotected fingers. One trick some of us have used is to sketch by gasoline lantern in the daytime, using the lantern as a hand warmer. Pencil, charcoal and pastel chalks lend themselves readily to winter sketching. Oils can be used under some circumstances but the finished painting is difficult to pack without smearing.

We seek out a sunlit spot out of the wind where we sit, light up the lantern and place it between our legs so that the heat from the top of it will drift up around the sketch pad on our knees. Then we sketch in spurts, making careful observations of form before committing our sketching hand to the cold. When the hand begins to stiffen, we put it under the sketch pad above the lantern where it will warm up.

It is necessary to "fix" charcoal or pastel once a sketch is completed. For this we use a small can of ordinary hair spray which we keep inside our parka where body warmth will prevent it from freezing up. Some painters use cameras to catch a particular scene, then make a rough pencil drawing of the same scene with marginal notes on color and other details. Back home at the studio, they use the photo and drawing to make the final sketch and painting.

REPAIRS TO EQUIPMENT

Considerable time in camp is taken up with checking equipment and repairing any damage. Clothing rips are sewn up, straps, lacings, tent ropes and fabrics gone over. We carry a repair kit made up of a coil of soft wire, needles and thread, thimble, a roll of plumber's duct tape, pliers and nylon lacing all rolled up in a square of ripstop nylon cloth which can be cut up for patching. Glue does not work well in the cold and we don't bother to carry it.

KEEPING UP THE JOURNAL

One of the last items of the day's business is to make the final entry in the trip log. We record not only the trip's progress and highlights, but also any specific observations on equipment and methods which can be revised after the trip. And then we blow out the candle, draw the hood tight around our face, bury ourselves in the delicious fluffy warmth of the bag and drift off into the dreamless, relaxing sleep of the outdoors.

EPILOGUE

None of the foregoing is intended to be the final word on winter camping. That book has not yet been written. It may never be

written. As long as the human species inhabits this planet and as long as there exists somewhere a cold climate, there will be people meeting the challenge of living in the snow, studying it, travelling in it, devising better methods and equipment for coping with it . . . and thoroughly enjoying it. As it has been throughout history, this great adventure will always be reserved for those hardy souls who thrill to the challenge of a breathtaking, whistling north wind, are awed by the sheer grandeur of the winter landscape and have an insatiable curiosity to see what is beyond that next snow-capped ridge.

APPENDIX: I

EQUIPMENT CHECK LIST

Group Items

Tents and flies, poles, ropes, anchors—extra nylon tarps (10 × 12)
Sleds and backpacks
Sleeping bags and mats
Snow shovel
Ice chisel, ice skimmer
Repair kit
First aid kit
Toilet paper, paper towels
Skis, snowshoes, poles, extra ski tips, ski wax
Cook pot, bowls, spoons, cups, utensils, can opener

Stove and fuel, funnel
Flashlight, extra batteries
Matches in waterproof containers
Extra ¼-inch and ⅛-inch rope
Soft wire
Needlenose pliers
Duct tape
Fishing tackle
Fillet knife
Saw
Lantern and mantles

Personal Items

Map, compass
Matches
Pocket knife
Sunglasses or goggles
Water bottle
Toothbrush
Shaving gear, metal mirror
Soap, washcloth, towel
Chapstick, suntan lotion

Camera
Film
Candle to read by
Books
Notebook
Sewing kit
Watch
Emergency ration
Kerchief

Clothing

Wind parka
Insulated camp parka
Wool trail pants
Wind pants
Insulated camp pants
Wool shirt
Two sets long underwear

Mittens and liners
Ski boots
Mukluks or pacs and liners
Sweater
Wool cap, earflapper cap
Face mask
At least two pair wool socks

APPENDIX: II

THREE-DAY MENU FOR FOUR PERSONS

First Day

Breakfast

Instant oatmeal
(individual packets)—8
Dry milk, sugar
Dry fruit cocktail—7 oz.
Tang (individual packets)—4
Coffee (instant, packets)—8

Lunch

Chicken soup (Cup-o'-Soup)—8
Rye Krisp
Squeeze packets
  peanut butter—8
Squeeze packets jelly—8
Instant chocolate—8
Cookies—8

Second Day

Breakfast

Eggs (precooked, scrambled,
  frozen in individual foil
  servings)—4 pkgs
Tang—4 pkgs.
Coffee—8 pkgs.
Fruit bars—4

Lunch

Pea Soup (Cup-o'-soup)—8
Rye Krisp
Sausage—12 oz.
Chocolate—8 pkgs.
Candy

Supper

Canned meat—two 12-oz. cans
Bannock (thawed by the fire)—1
Soft oleo
Mixed vegetables (precooked, frozen)—16-oz.
Instant, no-cook blueberry cobbler—11-oz. packet
Instant tea (individual packets)—8

Supper

Beef stroganoff (dry, instant)—18 oz.
Pilot biscuits (precooked, dry)—12
Oleo
Squeeze packet jelly—8
Instant, no-cook pudding—5¾ oz.
Coffee or tea—8

Third Day

Breakfast

Granola—12 oz.
   (3 oz. per person)
Instant dry milk
Sugar
Instant dry applesauce—8 oz.
Tang—4 packets
Coffee—8 packets

Lunch

Tomato soup (Cup-o'-Soup)—8
Cheese—12-oz. (or 4 oz. dry
   cheese spread)
Rye Krisp
Chocolate—8
Candy bars—4

Supper

Retort beef—4
Instant potatoes—6 cups dry
Instant milk

Oleo
Raspberry cobbler—11-oz. pkg.
Coffee or tea—8 pkgs.

Additional Kitchen Items

Salt
Pepper
Any other preferred seasoning
Wax paper

Paper towelling (optional)
Asbestos mitt
Tin foil

APPENDIX: III

WINTER CAMPING EQUIPMENT SUPPLIERS

Alpine Designs
6185 E. Arapahoe
P.O. Box 3407
Boulder, Colo. 80303

Eddie Bauer
Seattle, Wash. 98124

L. L. Bean
875 Main St.
Freeport, Me. 04032

Bill Bentley
Box 786
Tupper Lake, N.Y. 12986

Cabela's
812 13th Ave.
P.O. Box 199
Sidney, Neb. 69162

Camp 7
3245 Prairie Ave.
Boulder, Colo. 80302

Camp Trails
P.O. Box 14500-7
Phoenix, Ariz. 85063

Don Gleason's Campers Supply,
    Inc.
20 Pearl St.
Northampton, Mass. 01060

Eastern Mountain Sports
Vose Farm Rd.
Peterborough, N.H. 03458

Eureka Tent, Inc.
625 Conklin Rd.
Binghamton, N.Y. 13902

Frostline
452 Burbank
Broomfield, Colo. 80020

Gerry
5450 N. Valley Highway
Denver, Colo. 80216

Himalayan Industries, Inc.
P.O. Box 5668
Pine Bluff, Ark. 71601

Hirsch-Weis
5203 S.E. Johnson Creek Blvd.
Portland, Ore. 07206

Holubar
Box 7
Boulder, Colo. 80302

Kelty
1801 Victory Blvd.
Glendale, Ca. 91201

Nord Hus Sleds
P.O. Box 4
Togo, Minn. 55788

The North Face
Box 2399, Station A
Berkeley, Ca. 94702

Olam Outdoor Sports Products
Spring Hope, N.C. 27822

Oregon Freeze Dry Foods, Inc.
P.O. Box 1048
Albany, Ore. 97321

Paul Petzoldt Wilderness Equipment
Box 78 W
Lander, Wyo. 82520

Recreational Equipment, Inc.
1525 11th Ave.
Seattle, Wash. 98122

Refrigi-Wear, Inc.
Inwood, N.Y. 11696

Rich-Moor
P.O. Box 2728
Van Nuys, Ca. 91404

Sierra Designs
4th & Addison Sts.
Berkeley, Ca. 94710

Sierra Kits
P.O. Box 814
Riverside, Ca. 92515

Ski Hut
1615 University Ave.
Berkeley, Ca. 94703

Snowline Corp.
1330 9th St.
Berkeley, Ca. 94710

Trailtech
10 W. 33rd St.
New York, N.Y. 10001

Waters, Inc.
111 E. Sheridan St.
Ely, Minn. 55731

Index

Shelter, snow, 28–9 (*ill.* 26, 27)
Sketching, 124–5
Sleds. *See* Cross-country sled
Sleeping bags, 54 (*ill.* 45)
  care of, 43, 44–5, 82
  combination bags, 37–8
  design and construction, 34–5, 38–40
    (*ill.* 33)
  fasteners, 39–40
  fill, 35–8
  half bags, 40–1
  mats, 41–2, 45, 82
Snowshoes, 3, 11
  test run, 74
  with sled, 12
Snow conditions, 90–2 (*ill.* 92)
Sommers, Charles, Wilderness Canoe
    Base, Minnesota, vii–viii
Synthetic fibers, 36–8

Tents
  care of, 82
  converting summer, 27
  designs and materials, 22–4
  insulation, 27–8
  location, 18–19

pitching, 18–19, 21–2
preparing site, 19–20
prices, 26–7
sizes and weights, 24–7
Toboggans, 7–8
Toilet, 32–3 (*ill.* 32)
Tourist associations, 76
Trapp Family Lodge (Vermont), 6

U.S. Geological Survey, 74–5

Water
  consumption, 103–4
  drinking, 63
  sources, 95
Wind-Chill. *See under* Hazards
Winter Camping, vii–viii
  attitude, 3
  defined, 2
  ethics, 4
  itinerary, 80
  planning for, 70–80
  related activities, 121–6
  skills, 2–3
  See also Equipment